Bonnie,

I hope you enjoy reading this as much as I did writing it !

Shared Spaces

Sandra Lefever

Shared Spaces

An Innkeeper's Story with Recipes

by

Sandra Lefever

Kindle Direct Publishing

ISBN-9798654528704

Cover design by Karen Schotsch
Acorn Marketing & Advertising

Prologue

In the fall of 1996 we purchased a home in Geneva and moved from the farmhouse into town. This was the fulfillment of a long held dream to own one of the older homes we had admired for many years. We had no plans to do anything with our new residence other than to make it our home. Little did we know that the divine designer had a much bigger plan in mind. A year later we welcomed guests into our home, and our perspective of life changed completely. Everything happens for a reason. There are no coincidences.

TABLE OF CONTENTS

A turn of the century photo of the early years of the Charles Sloan family occupancy shows the original balcony and wrap-around porch. (Photo courtesy of the Kathryn Sloan Ashby family)

A local artist's drawing shows structural changes to the front of the house. (Drawing courtesy of the Hugh and Barb Wilkins family)

History of the Residents

1888-1892	John A. and Flora Dempster, builders
1892-1894	Flora Dempster
1894-1898	Asa F. and Arobine H. Cogswell
1898-1948	Charles H. and Emma Sloan
1948-1954	Fred W. and Ruth L. Underwood
1954-1959	James F. and Mary B. McCarthy
1959-1972	Ivan B. and Phyllis J. Nicholson
1972-1991	Charles F. and Pat Grothe
1991-1996	Scott and Libby J. Brettman (both had businesses in the home)
1996-2016	Ken and Sandy Lefever
1997-2012	Operated as Dempster Woods Bed and Breakfast

After getting established as a bed and breakfast, we averaged around 150 rooms per year. In the beginning we rented rooms for $45 and $55 including breakfast. We eventually raised the rates to $55 and $65, which many guests thought was very reasonable. Bridge and book club meeting rates, including a dessert, were $50 for the afternoon. Group home tours were free. Making money was never a motivating factor. The opportunity to "share the spaces" was paramount in this adventure. It enriched our lives.

1. Whose Plan Is It?

The summer was more than half over when the doorbell rang at 3:30 one especially steamy afternoon.

I opened the door.

Two women greeted me, "Is this a bed and breakfast?"

My first instinct was to reply, "No, you must have the wrong house."

When my husband Ken and I had impulsively purchased this house the previous year, we immediately began to talk about and plan for the day we would welcome guests. Unfortunately, or fortunately, depending on one's perspective, romanticizing this scenario did not prepare me for its reality. I had envisioned being physically and mentally prepared when those longed for guests stood on our threshold for the first time. I hadn't expected them to be two heat-bedraggled drop-ins. Nor had I ever planned to welcome anyone in a "George Killian Irish Red" T-shirt with a stretched out neck. When had anyone ever seen me wearing something that promoted alcohol?

After several long seconds, I finally acknowledged the question.

"Yes, it is. Come in." I then wondered what to do next.

No problem. Mary, the blond-haired younger of the two ladies, took charge.

"Do you have a room available?" she asked.

"Yes. You are our first guests." Not exactly a professional approach.

"How did you come here?"

I really hadn't intended it to sound like I thought a UFO had dropped them off.

"We asked at the dress shop if there was a bed and breakfast in town and then drove all over town trying to find it. We were looking for it east of the highway instead of west, but we finally found it. You don't have a sign," Mary informed me.

"Well, we have a room, but my husband was just in the process of putting a shower head over the tub in the bathroom, so you won't be able to take a shower."

Was I trying to talk them out of staying?

This time the tiny, gray-haired, older lady added her two cents, "Oh, I prefer a bathtub anyway."

Mary agreed.

Our guests had solved my dilemma of what to do next.

"May we see the room?" Mary asked.

We headed up the open staircase into the upstairs heat. The older lady looked about the same age as my 75-year-old mother, who couldn't have tolerated the oppressive heat and humidity upstairs for even a few minutes. If I had expected guests, I would have turned on the upper level air conditioner in advance of their arrival. This was not how I had envisioned such a momentous occasion.

"How much is the room?"

"Oh, I don't know. We haven't really decided---$45?"

I couldn't remember exactly how the discussion about room rates between my husband and me had ended. What a businesswoman! The slight hesitation of our potential guests seemed like an eternity. Who could blame them?

"Do you want to stay here, Vera?" Mary asked her companion.

I felt like a criminal, awaiting the jury's verdict. Given my initial uncertainty about our preparedness for guests, wasn't I a little overly concerned about the outcome? Would our future as innkeepers depend on Vera's response?

"It's all right," she answered.

"I'll start the air conditioner to cool your room, and I need to get the bathroom ready," I added in an uncertain, apologetic tone.

Since I needed time to prepare their room, I proceeded to tell them about a restaurant in a little town nine miles away.

Mary was very perceptive. She suggested that they return at 7:00.

"Would that give you enough time?" she asked.

I agreed that would work, wondering who was really in charge.

Mary offered to write their names and addresses in a guest book as is usually done in these establishments. We had no guestbook yet, so I grabbed a pad of post-it-notes and a pen for her use. Miraculously, I had the presence of mind to give her our phone number and draw a map to the restaurant. Obviously, I had a lot to learn as an innkeeper!

Our decision to open a bed and breakfast had been almost as impulsive as the purchase of this home. The real estate company's photo in the county newspaper was accompanied by the words "potential bed and breakfast." We made our decision like some parents who decide to have a child, enthralled with the idea, but oblivious to the practicalities.

Six years previously we had viewed the property with no serious intentions of purchasing it. Its condition at that time and the stage of our lives were factors in our decision to remain on the farm a few more years.

My husband, who can put a positive spin on any situation, merely observed, "Maybe whoever buys it will renovate it and then put it up for sale again!"

Six years later our second tour of the home revealed many significant improvements and a higher price tag. The timing was right. We made an offer. While Ken returned to daily routine unaffected by the uncertain outcome, I agonized until the bidding process was completed. In a matter of a few days, we learned that we would finally own one of the historic homes in our community. For me, the sleepless nights began.

I love to imagine, to plan, to problem-solve. I pondered the dilemma of converting from a predominantly blue color scheme to the mauve/rose setting of the common rooms in the 1887 Italianate. I paged through catalogs, looking for a quilt that would blend with the Victorian doll wallpaper in one of the bedrooms. Would one of my homemade quilts from the farmhouse be suitable? Prone in my bed, I virtually hung pictures and moved and rearranged more furniture in one dark night than a moving company in a month.

Each morning I awakened exhausted, but the dreaming didn't stop. I waited impatiently for a closing date. It was a delicious torture to rely only on my memory of those brief moments in each of the twelve rooms. I visualized my piano on one of the library walls. I fretted that the fabric on our sofa would clash with the existing floral carpet.

One day, unable to resist stopping at the house, I stood on the porch and curved my hand over my brow to peer through the lace curtains into the parlor window. Although the urge to peek into each of the eleven remaining seven-foot, ground-floor windows was overpowering, I resisted.

Every morning as I whizzed by "M" street on the way to my teaching job, I craned my neck to catch a passing glimpse of our soon-to-be home. It was still there, waiting. Like me.

After work one glorious Indian summer afternoon, I treated myself to an ice cream cone and pulled into the driveway on "M" street. The scene before me resembled an artist's canvas. Eager to satisfy my impatient longing for full owner's rights, I climbed out of the car, shuffled through the rustling leaves in my path, and stepped onto the canvas. Cone in hand, I perched on the top step of the wrap-around porch, licking and thinking about the day we would finally unlock the door and once again step inside.

I engaged in a captivating fantasy, which filled my days and my nights, my conscious and my sub-conscious. It challenged my practical nature and jump-started my creativity. How had this happened? Whose plan was it?

*   *   *   *   *   *

"Thank you, thank you, for allowing my aunt and I to share your home, for allowing us to be your first guests. I feel that we would be good friends if we lived in the same town." **North Platte, Nebraska**

"May the Lord bless you and your home as you continue to serve and bless so many!" **Gothenburg, Nebraska**

2. Preserving the Past

We have spent most of our lives in older homes, some by destiny, some by choice. Our first home was a $70 per month, older rental property which already had inhabitants. A large colony of mice hung out in an old upright piano and under the burners of the gas stove. The day I made eye contact with a mouse in a drawer among the kitchen towels, necessity became the mother of invention. Ken mounted a pegboard on the kitchen wall for hanging pots and pans. This was the first item on what became a lengthy list of "old house" coping strategies.

Our first furnishings were in "early relative" style. What we perceived as our parents' generosity may have been a convenient solution to growing collections in their basements. Among them were a wooden bed, prone to collapse without an old typewriter case holding up one corner, a dark green, vinyl, fold-down couch with a storage compartment underneath (another place for mice), and a very weathered, drop leaf table retrieved from Ken's parents' storm cave.

With an abundance of youthful enthusiasm and a modest amount of ingenuity, we proceeded to make the mouse haven a homey, human retreat. Ken antiqued our bed headboard and an old, upright piano. He refinished my grandmother's Duncan Phyfe coffee table. I ordered a J. C. Penney slipcover for the "antique futon" and sewed curtains for the living room windows. Our first real antiques joined this eclectic group of furnishings. The price was right because few people wanted antiques in the 1960s. Grandma Lilly advised me as I bid on an auction item for the first time in Milligan, Nebraska. Eleven dollars was a small price to pay for an oak, secretary desk, still one of my favorite pieces.

Four years later we finally escaped from life in the "mouse house" and moved into our newly constructed, split level home. Ken had done the finishing work, and I had made new curtains and created my first set of lined draperies. Since we lived in this home such a short time, there were very few memorable moments. Unless one counts Ken's failure to catch our 11-month-old son jumping to him on the stairway.

"Now, how did you say this happened?" queried the emergency room doctor for the second time as he stitched the gash above our toddler's eyebrow.

After living in our new multi-level home for only eighteen months, Ken retired from teaching and coaching. We had experienced life in a spacious, new, mouse-proof home. It hadn't delivered. The laundry, TV room, kitchen, and bedrooms were each on a different floor. Three sets of stairs and young children were a challenging combination. No traces of former owners, no house history, and no noteworthy, esthetic appeal came with that home.

Without the engaging diversion of an old home's history, new home owners can spend more time lamenting the first dent on a cupboard door or wishing they had chosen a different floor plan. In the renovation process, the new owner of an older property must adapt somewhat to its blueprint and think "outside of the box." Whatever its vintage, each home becomes what the owners make it: a fulfilled dream and/or a living history.

We were prepared to add to the history of another older house in our hometown of Geneva, where Ken began to farm with his father. A house hunt on a tight budget turned up a 1920 Craftsman bungalow in my childhood neighborhood. Many years ago I had sat on the long, oak window seat in this home's dining room. There I visited with Florence, an elderly spinster, as she tatted around a linen handkerchief. She enthusiastically supplied the history behind each of the elephants in her extensive collection. The elephants had long since disappeared from the bookcase room dividers, but nothing else in the house had changed. It desperately needed to be updated.

Ken refinished oak woodwork and floors, replaced old tile, closed a doorway, and remodeled the kitchen. We painted and papered walls and carpeted some of the rooms. I hung newly sewn red and white, gingham curtains in the dining room above the window seat and lined draperies in the living room.

Then I insisted we address the bathroom issue. Years of heeding my mother's warning not to sit on a public toilet without lining the seat with paper had developed into a full-fledged phobia. My elderly friend Florence had died on the toilet. Fear overcame frugality. We replaced the toilet. With the purchase of this home, we had the opportunity to add to the presence of Florence's spirit and leave our own "thumbprints."

Life in an older home is like opening an anecdotal, history book filled with former owners' stories. The desiccated condoms hidden in basement floor joists, the musty, old books stored in a chest freezer, the endearing imperfection of crookedly carved letters in a child's hand on a cupboard door were all catalysts for lively conversations and some serious speculation about former residents.

After four years of uncovering "stories" in our Craftsman bungalow, we exchanged dwellings with Ken's parents. Each of our childhood homes was built in the 1920s by our grandparents who had passed them on to our parents. Now we were the new owners of the Lefever family farmhouse.

Our first day on the farm was November 7, 1977. We awoke to a blizzard, closed schools, a well that had ceased to function, and an abundance of flies from moving day. An ominous introduction to country living for this city girl!

If the walls in old homes could talk, what would they say? Would they reveal secrets about the previous owners? Yes. Would they pose a question: "Don't you know that the only thing that works in an old house is the owner?" Yes.

In spite of the challenges, we were intent on updating the farmhouse. This involved major structural changes: the transformation of the kitchen into a utility room/bathroom and the dining room into a kitchen. These ambitious projects in a third generation "family" home created more physical and emotional stress than is healthy for anyone. A life with mounds of plaster, laths, sawdust, and three young children tested our patience. Ken's mother's reactions to the renovations provided an additional opportunity for personal growth. She frequently reminded us of the way the house used to be. She had been unable to make any changes in her in-laws' former home.

In addition to the special dynamics of a daughter-in-law and a mother-in-law making changes in each other's former homes, there is a palpable presence of all the souls who ever lived there. These character-filled homes connect the cultures of the generations who have shared the same spaces. While some house hunters see unappealing, awkward, outdated living quarters which require too much work, others, like us, see possibilities and the converging personalities of the former and present occupants. Each home tells its story. Our passion was to collect and preserve the best parts of a home's history and to create a few more chapters of our own.

Little did we know that an even older home with its own idiosyncrasies would appear on the distant horizon, one with a parade of people in its past and many more in its future. More history and more renovations awaited us.

*　　*　　*　　*　　*　　*

"Your place is so unique and it is wonderful to know that people like you care enough to preserve a part of the heritage of our country." **Omaha, Nebraska**

3. Claim It and Name It

Everything farmers do is based on the changing seasons. At the end of a long harvest season in the fall, many things happen. Farmers wash their combines and their cars. They make large purchases: a new vehicle, a new home. They move to town.

Nineteen years after a November move to the farm, we returned to town, also in November. We had intended to move only the large items while extended family visited. Our sons had a different idea. Even though we had more household goods than in our previous moves, they wanted to move everything while extra bodies were available. It was an admirable undertaking to accomplish in one weekend.

My task was twofold: inform the heavy lifters where to place the furniture and help my sisters put away the breakables. After everyone had left, we soon discovered that our helpers hadn't moved everything. Where were our toothbrushes? I made a quick trip to the farmhouse to retrieve personal items left behind in the bathroom drawers. The statue of Mary, my Blessed Mother, had also been left behind in the garden. I would retrieve her another day when I said my last good-by to country living.

Of course, in spite of the disorganized surroundings, both of us left for work on Monday morning. For weeks we hunted through boxes for items we needed or wanted, like Ken's dress shoes.

Soon the Christmas season was upon us. While nothing had changed for Ken, the thought of a Victorian Christmas in a Victorian house intoxicated me. When the excitement of our first Christmas in our new home had worn off, with very little thought or discussion, we decided to open a bed and breakfast.

We didn't arrive at this life-altering decision by asking ourselves logical, thoughtful questions. Is it economically feasible? What impact will it have on our personal lives? Our questions were more like those asked by parents who learn they are expecting a baby. What shall we call it? Should we opt for a familiar name or invent one? Some psychologists claim that the name chosen for one's child may determine the personality. We mulled over ideas until we realized that our "baby" already had a personality. In fact, two of them.

When a large limestone rock etched with "Dempster Woods" appeared on our lawn, some members of our small community were puzzled. What was the reason for that choice? It was a well-known fact that the home's longest residents were Charles and Emma Sloan, who occupied it for fifty years. Older Genevans usually referred to it as the "Sloan House." A Sloan descendant told us that the Sloan family traditionally gathered around the flagpole every Fourth of July to sing the National Anthem, perhaps somewhere in the vicinity of our rock. Since there was a mausoleum bearing the Sloan name in the public cemetery, we decided not to call it the "Sloan House."

A walk down Geneva's main street to admire the old storefronts provides the first clue to our name choice. "Dempster's Block 1887" appears on one of the original storefronts. It was there that John A. Dempster and his brother began a business which provided general merchandise, drugs, and notions.

Before making a home in Nebraska, Dempster served in the Illinois Volunteer Infantry and participated in seventeen Civil War battles. After moving to Fillmore County, Nebraska, in addition to his store, he was responsible for the organization of public school districts in the county, served as a postmaster and a state legislator, ran for governor, and became the first president of the Geneva National Bank. Our home sits on a portion of the eighty acres Dempster purchased on the north edge of Geneva. The land was developed into three separate additions to the city. Our property was located in the third addition.

In 1887, the same year Dempster moved into his new home and entered politics, Sloan passed his bar exam. As the county attorney and a popular orator, Sloan delivered the oration at the laying of the cornerstone of the new Fillmore County Courthouse in 1893. He had been First Orator of his class at the State Agricultural College in Ames, Iowa. There he also won numerous debates, edited the college newspaper, played baseball, and belonged to a fraternity. He also played a role in government as a Nebraska state senator and a member of the U. S. Congress.

The contributions of these two prominent, public figures were factors in "Dempster Woods" being listed on the National Register of Historic Places in 2005. One criterion met was "property is associated with the lives of persons significant in our past." Its official historic name "Dempster-Sloan House" was one we had considered and rejected for our business. It sounded too much like a funeral home.

While Ken assembled research to complete the data for the National Register, I accidentally ran across a spiral bound book entitled *The Dempsters* in the reference section of the Geneva Public Library. The following day, February 14, Ken received a unique Valentine gift, photocopies of the Dempsters' family story.

While Dempster had much success in some of his endeavors, he was not so fortunate in his personal life. After living in the new home only four years, his wife Flora shared her memories in a letter to their children in 1892.

> I cannot recall how many years we lived there (first home in Geneva) when again your father wished to improve more and more and he bought an eighty acre farm adjoining the town site, and laid off a part of the town lots, and built a large two story brick house, a very fine home . . .we all enjoyed the country like place with beautiful trees and lawn. . .You were not all in this home, all the time as in the other . . .Your father finally sold his merchants business and invested . . . I am sorry to say that misfortune followed the exchange in business, and unpleasant things grew and multiplied in our marriage relations, as the result of my condition of health; and finally as you all know too well, resulted in the tragedy of separation, which is the saddest and most deplorable thing that can be.

We hoped our inn would provide happier memories than those recorded by Flora Dempster. In order to attract guests, our next step was to create a brochure which featured the guest rooms. Naming the bed and breakfast had not been nearly as much fun as creating names for these four rooms. My imagination and excitement kicked into high gear. It was like naming quadruplets! Each room possessed distinguishing characteristics.

Above the large, southern-facing window in what had been Sloan's rather small master bedroom was a decorative transom of multi-colored stained glass panes. We purchased an antique door with similar glass panes. This door opened to what had been Emma Sloan's dressing room, now a bathroom.

Guests awakened to the shimmering of glass panes and an eclectic array of colorful prints on the steel blue walls. We named the room "Rainbow's End."

The largest bedroom had a three window bay. Its architecture called for something more dramatic and sophisticated. A magazine photo of a room in a small French chateau inspired the décor of "French Connections." Deep, rich, red walls, accented with hand-stamped, gold fleur-de-lis above the picture rail, created an elegant old-world appeal. Imagine the Sloans' choice to make this the children's room, which they called "the dormitory." It had an exit door which led onto an upper story balcony! A tempting opportunity for their children to explore!

The "Demoiselle Room" owed its name to the Victorian doll wallpaper and my preoccupation with all things French ("demoiselle" is French for young miss). Eastlake period furnishings, a very "early relative" bedroom set originally owned by Ken's great-grandparents, and an antique sewing machine provided old-fashioned charm. A relative of Charles Sloan supplied us with a bit of humorous trivia for this room. It was the site of his conception.

The only guest room with a view of Dempster's woods was a whimsical child's retreat. "Alice's Window-on-the-Woods" became a wonderland of stuffed animals, an ancestral youth bed, birdhouses suspended from the ceiling, and butterfly-shaped wallpaper cutouts on one wall. Although there was no evidence that either family had employed a maid, guests liked to think that this tiny room must have been the maid's.

Alas! I had one regret after naming and decorating the four guestrooms. There were no more.

* * * * * *

"A very special treat to spend the weekend in Bill's grandparents' home! The upstairs front closet brings back special memories of playing with his grandfather's Masonic sword and of ceiling height stacks of National Geographics. The grandchildren loved climbing the big pine tree." **Grants Pass, Oregon**

"Mylicent and I enjoyed ourselves. It was especially nice for me to remember that when she was much younger than I am, my grandmother lived

in this house for a period of time." **LeMars, Iowa**
   "Beautiful snow covered walk in the woods!" **Anonymous**

4. Sleeping Around

Beds. We provided them in every size: two antique double beds and one antique youth bed, all requiring custom mattresses, one queen, one king, one antique futon, one contemporary futon, and one sofa bed. Enough beds to sleep seventeen people or more on the first and second floors, depending on how well acquainted they were. That also meant a lot of laundry!

All these beds did not migrate from the farmhouse. The king, actually twin mattresses on twin frames, belonged originally to my grandparents (my grandmother had died in one of them). The versatility of being able to convert from a king to twins provided more options for guests. We purchased the sofa bed at a garage sale and the antique futon at an antique store.

Beds weren't the only "housewarming gifts." An antique sewing machine and two antique rockers from Ken's mother, a chamber pot, Fostoria dessert plates, and a print of St. Cecilia from the old parish rectory added to the Victorian feel. St. Cecilia, a patron saint of music, hung appropriately above the piano.

It's a good idea for innkeepers to be guests in their own inn and to sleep on every bed in every guestroom at some point in time. Yes, I have even slept on the futon in the north room of the ground floor (originally the home's kitchen). In the early years it served as our evening getaway from guests. The futon, a wood-burning stove, and a television made it a cozy retreat. It was also the most accessible bed for my two-month recovery from a broken ankle. Guests with mobility issues preferred this option over a real bed at the top of the steep stairs.

Spending the night in a room is really the best way to discover if it will appeal to guests. Is the bedside lighting adequate for those who read? Is the alarm user friendly? Are the pillows too soft or too hard? Does too much light come through the windows in the morning? Is the temperature comfortable? Does the room smell fresh? Neglect in any of these areas might render a less than perfect comment on the Nebraska Association of Bed and Breakfast comment card supplied to guests.

Guests could literally get lost in our upstairs and find it challenging to navigate their way from the back to the front of the house. Front and back stairways led to two separate hallways. When we opened for business, the upstairs had only one bathroom. It was just off the back hallway at the north end of the house. Three of the rooms had access to this hall and bathroom. In order to use this bath, guests in the front bedroom and front hall had to walk through one of the two bedrooms in the center of the upstairs. These centrally located bedrooms each had a front and a back door. For that reason we initially didn't book "Rainbow's End," the front bedroom. When guests reserved "French Connections," which was our bedroom at that time, we migrated to "Rainbow's End."

Remember that game show in which the participant had to choose door number one, two, or three? That was the dilemma in both hallways when the doors were closed.

An example of this occurred one evening when two sisters had reserved the king bed in "French Connections." One of them lived in Geneva and wanted to escape from her own house guests. We had left the front door unlocked and gone to bed in "Rainbow's End." The sisters tiptoed upstairs and came directly into door number one where we were sleeping. Although many bed and breakfast guests don't lock their doors, locks in occupied rooms are sometimes helpful.

Another complication was the location of our clothes closet. It was not in our bedroom for two reasons. Guests would not have appreciated our need to retrieve clothing from their room. More importantly, that space was too small to hold many clothes. Emma Sloan's dressing room off the front hallway provided enough space for seasonal clothing and an ironing board. This proved to be a slightly inconvenient, workable arrangement for quite some time.

Our ability to be at ease with guests in our home ensured enjoyment on all sides, especially when they entered our bedroom in the dark of night. Hugs from guests who felt like family were always very satisfying. We wanted them to feel at home, but there were limits to this approach.

Several days into a female minister's week-long stay with us, Ken came home during the day to shower and change clothes. Farmers sometimes find it necessary to "clean up" at unpredictable times. It goes with the lifestyle. He showered in the ground floor bathroom off the kitchen and headed up the backstairs, intending to walk through one of the inner bedrooms to our closet in the front hall to get a new set of clothes. This was a better choice than going up the front stairs. In a few seconds he appeared downstairs "au naturel."

"What are you doing?" I asked.

"I went up to get some clothes," he replied. "When I heard footsteps on the front stairs, I remembered that we have a guest."

If this surprise encounter had actually materialized, it would not have ruffled his feathers one bit. On the other hand, an encounter with a naked man certainly would have given our guest, a female minister, some interesting material for next Sunday's sermon. This too-close-for-comfort situation provided me with a "Ken story" which I have shared many times.

Later the same day, I discovered that Ken, without consulting me, had transferred the closet's contents to the basement. Now we were sleeping upstairs, two floors away from our clothing. I had a premonition where our next bedroom would be.

*   *   *   *   *   *

"Your themes, decorating, and food are all very tasteful and time seemed to stand still for us as we soaked up your memories and stories." **Wahoo, Nebraska**

"The home, the room, and the décor are beautiful. I felt pampered as well as refreshed. We enjoyed a full moon and fireflies on the front porch. My husband came prepared with wine, cheese, and crackers. I will always treasure the memory of this anniversary and our stay here." **Gothenburg, Nebraska**

5. Our Place in History

"You have this beautiful, historic home and sleep in the basement," exclaimed many of our bed and breakfast guests when I answered the "Where's your bedroom?" query.

In an attempt to make light of our own living arrangements, I amused our guests with a painfully true explanation, "Yup! We're down in the basement with all the other projects and rejects."

I didn't elaborate on the multitude and magnitude of what else, besides us, was in the lowest level of our home. I allowed them a few moments to conjure up images of what an 1887 vintage basement probably looked like: dirt floor, cracking foundation, cobwebs, things creeping and scurrying to the darkest corners, especially when the light came on. I had always dreaded descending the stairs in our 1920 bungalow. Like octopus arms, the gigantic ducts of the old, coal furnace stretched toward the ceiling. As I filled the dryer and started another load of laundry, I was acutely aware of that motionless monstrosity which dominated the room. At least this basement didn't have one of those old furnaces.

We dispelled our guests' sense of horror when we told them that it was the basement that had motivated us to purchase the house. The previous owners had updated much in the home in six years, but the most impressive improvement was the elevation of it one inch for the installation of a new basement. We had the luxury of our own unfinished, private suite: a bedroom, a bathroom with a pedestal sink, a super-sized, clawfoot tub, and a walk-in closet.

There are blessings and curses to every situation. To reach our private place we passed through what realtors call the mechanical room, just outside our bedroom. At various intervals a new noise serenaded us through the night: a rumbling furnace, a churning water softener, a humming dehumidifier. A symphony of modern conveniences. It was nearly impossible to sleep through the roaring of the hot water heater in our bedroom. It fired up like a rocket lifting off the launching pad. Additionally, we heard every flushed toilet and the activation of the sump pump. Our guests were home!

Since our married life had begun in a basement apartment, perhaps it was significant that we had come full circle. However, the adjustment to new, nightly sounds had definitely been much easier thirty years ago. Our first basement dwelling had served only one purpose. It was a place to live. In the bed and breakfast, due to the unavailability of guest-bedroom storage, we shared our basement private quarters with an ever-changing and growing accumulation: antique furniture in a stalled stage of refinishing, fermenting wine to be bottled, tubs and drawers of fabric for quilt piecing, a cabinet of home-canned produce and canning supplies, a collection of "early relative" furniture no longer in use.

The preservation of family history was, and is, a predominate pattern of our lives. Surrounded by an enclosure of gray, concrete blocks, adorned with outdated family portraits from my mother's estate, we lay in the bed of Ken's youth, the same bed we had shared as newlyweds on visits to his parents' farm, the exact bed in which his grandmother had died many decades ago. (Unlike toilets, deathbeds have no impact on my mental well-being.)

It was from this ancestral place of permanent repose that I scrutinized the latest, feeble attempt to improve the ambiance of our surroundings: a homemade quilt, suspended along the north wall. My brain explored options for the unfinished ceiling. I could drape and staple yards of gauzy fabric to the century-plus floor joists. I could threaten to move upstairs and sleep alone. I could risk Ken's disapproval by commissioning a carpenter. Finally, I settled for just closing my eyes to imagine an elaborate, tin ceiling like the ones in the rest of the house. With my eyes closed I could no longer see the maze of PVC pipe, electrical wires, phone lines, heat ducts, vents, and cobwebs which reappeared as we slept.

"Ding dong!" The doorbell interrupted me from my reverie. I had forgotten to leave the front door unlocked for our guests' late return from a family reunion. I bounded up the steps to the second dong of the bell.

"You said you would leave the door unlocked," was the simultaneous greeting.

I opened the door and twelve people trickled in. A group of large guests, mostly males, filled the parlor. Some carried guitar cases. They introduced themselves. The last "man" was a shaggy-haired, 25-year-old specimen of arrested adolescence, wearing a backwards baseball cap. Dressed in long, baggy, denim shorts and an equally baggy, red T-shirt, he carried his black backpack into the library. He removed cigarettes and Black Sabbath compact discs from the backpack and placed them on the coffee table.

A counted cross stitch biblical verse hung on the stair landing. It flashed before me. "Do not neglect hospitality, for through it some have entertained angels."

"Excuse me," I said in a tone as politely assertive as possible. "Do you know you can't smoke in here?"

Chords erupted from the piano in the parlor. The two largest men retrieved guitars from cases. In a matter of seconds, several others gathered around the piano and joined their voices to the music. As I stood in my red and black, checkered, flannel robe with wet hair from a shower, I caught my husband's look across the dining room. Our eyes conveyed the twin thoughts in our heads: another historic moment at Dempster Woods.

"Good night, everyone. See you in the morning."

We escaped down the steps to our basement refuge.

I thought of the cigarettes on the coffee table and muttered, "I hope the house doesn't burn down while we are sleeping."

Ken turned out the light as we cuddled in the relatively quiet comfort of his grandmother's deathbed.

*   *   *   *   *   *

"It was comforting to know that after a long drive across the prairie, there was a key left for me to come in to a cozy room and sleep." **St. Paul, Minnesota**

"Thank you for sharing your lovely home and for the fellowship. This will be one stay in Geneva I won't forget." **McCool Junction, Nebraska**

6. It's Not Like That in France!

Why did our inn have a French theme? Because I am a Francophile: a person who loves all things French. The first French "thing" I loved was my future husband. He came with an irresistible, authentic ancestry, including a family coat of arms. What woman in her right mind could resist that?

Ken's ancestor, George Newton LeFevre, had compiled a genealogical record of the descendants of Abraham LeFevre. Included in his book, The Pennsylvania LeFevres, is the family history. In 1685, like many other Huguenots (a newly formed Protestant religion), the LeFevre family became victims of persecution by the Roman Catholic Church in France. Abraham's entire family was martyred, except for his sixteen-year-old son Isaac. With his father's Bible concealed in a loaf of bread, Isaac fled from France to Bavaria in Germany with Daniel Ferree, a French nobleman. While there he married Daniel's daughter Catherine. They eventually migrated to England where Queen Anne welcomed religious refugees. With the queen's assistance and William Penn's promise of a tract of land in Pennsylvania, the family set sail for America. Twenty-seven years after his escape, Isaac, Catherine, and their two sons arrived at the site of their new home. Seeing their new land, they named it "Paradise" (Paradise, Pennsylvania).

Ken is a ninth generation descendant of Isaac. In 1968 it was my privilege to accompany Ken to Paradise where we visited the LeFevre Cemetery and viewed Isaac's Bible in a museum in Lancaster, Pennsylvania.

In our own home years later, Ken received an unexpected privilege related to this piece of history. As I gave some Catholic nuns a tour of our house, I couldn't resist telling them Isaac's story and calling their attention to the Huguenot cross Ken was wearing.

One of the nuns knelt before Ken on the oak floor and exclaimed, "Please forgive us!"

The second French thing I fell for was the language. As a German major in college, I decided to take a French class just for the fun of it. It was "love at first sound." Compared to guttural German, its lyrical, musical quality was like riding gentle, rhythmical waves. Anything, and I mean anything, sounds heavenly in French. Even swear words like "merde" (pronounced mairt) sound much pleasanter than the German equivalent "Scheisse" (shy suh). After all, French is one of the Romance languages, a language of love. If only my French husband could speak more than a few French words.

I was so enamored with my third language that German was relegated to a minor course of study. With the completion of some French correspondence courses during the summer months, I earned a teaching endorsement in three years and began a thirty-year career of teaching German, French, English, and eventually Spanish.

Thanks to my students, the French culture was the third thing I fell in love with. They enriched my own cultural knowledge when they shared with the class anything French. Food was the most popular choice (no French fries or French toast). They could prepare something from a recipe booklet I provided or find their own recipes which I added to the booklet the next year. One student taught us the basics of French Impressionism. Her lesson inspired me to hang glossy, calendar prints of the masters (Monet, Renoir, Degas, and Gaughin) in our guest rooms. The second-year classes often prepared a French meal and served the school administrators. Following participation in the University of Nebraska foreign language fairs, we dined in the French Café in Omaha's Old Market. Bon appetit!

In an effort to enrich our lives with more French-based experiences, we hosted French exchange students in our home for short periods. This was another way to "bring American students out of the cornfield," as one college educator put it. As a mother of three sons, I had really hoped for a female student; however, as fate would have it, all three were males. In our family the males are not overly conversational. The addition of a silent stranger didn't improve the verbal exchange. A tense silence initially prevailed at some family meals.

One of these awkward evenings, I thought it would be a nice gesture to prepare a French meal. The main entrée was "coq au vin," chicken in wine sauce.

When I explained that we were having a French dinner, Xavier took his first dubious bite and proclaimed, "Ees not like zat een Frahns."

I reminded myself how blessed I was that this college agricultural student spent most of his time with Ken.

In spite of Xavier's rather ungracious receptiveness to my well-intended efforts to make him feel at home, we planned a July 4th barbecue and fireworks display for the 14th of July. This was Bastille Day, France's independence day. Unexpectedly, the fireworks began before the barbecue. Our sons' tent burst into flames, most likely from a misdirected firecracker. Ken's brother-in-law evacuated the tent of its contents: pillows, a boom box, and some sheepish-looking, young cousins whose lips are still sealed.

The cultural exchange was not as one-sided as I have made it seem. While they rogued the bean fields together, Xavier taught our sons French swear words which were not in this French teacher's vocabulary. They also learned that kilometers and miles are not equal. On a trip to the county fairgrounds, Xavier took the wheel because our sons weren't old enough to drive. He thought he was driving 70 kilometers per hour. His terrified passengers had never ridden that fast in the old pick-up.

We learned other things from our next two guests. Sylvain demonstrated how a real Frenchman makes crêpes. From our final student, Michael, we learned that having a foreigner in your family for more than a month can sometimes be too long when personalities don't exactly click.

At long last I finally accepted that one could only "Frenchify" oneself so much in the middle of America. The time had come to take the big leap, an excursion to a French-speaking country! Eight students, another sponsor, and I ventured abroad for the first time by not leaving North America. A trip to Québec seemed less intimidating because Canada is a bilingual country. It took a span of seven more years before I summoned the courage to sponsor students to France and England. Six years later in 2000 Ken and I traveled to France together for the first time.

Thanks to Sylvain's cooking demonstration, our inn's signature dish became crêpes. We also served Quiche Lorraine and Rustic Pear Tarts. On one very memorable occasion two married couples arrived for a French immersion weekend. The wives had surprised their husbands by taking them to an unknown destination. They requested that I speak French while we served them. They arrived with a fully equipped picnic basket and immediately proceeded to set the coffee table with a red and white, checkered tablecloth, wine, four goblets, and a corkscrew. The purpose of the getaway was to relive their travels together in France.

In the morning six Francophiles exchanged travel memories at breakfast. Exhilarating! It was a perfect weekend, except for the brown welcome mat. Army worms had attacked our lawn the night before their arrival. The hardy, green fescue had turned brown overnight.

"Can't you do something?" I pleaded with Ken, who could fix almost anything and did.

"What do you want me to do? Spray paint it green?"

As I recalled the pastoral vista of stone ruins and fresh greenness surrounding a centuries-old farmhouse in France's Loire Valley, I reminded him that it wasn't like that in France.

*   *   *   *   *   *

"This is one of the nicest B & B stays we've ever had. Seems like we've known you forever . . .Merci beaucoup pour le bon séjour et la bonne conversation." **Waverly, Iowa**

"It was a pleasure to stay here and rekindle memories of France. Your breakfasts were way more enjoyable than any we had in our four years in Paris!" **New Fairfield, Connecticut**

"I really enjoyed this room. It reminded me of my trip to Paris. I especially enjoyed the picture over the bed. The massage was terrific." **Omaha, Nebraska**

7. Enchantment

Part of the appeal of checking into a bed and breakfast is checking out of daily living. Upon arrival guests may be tired from a long day's drive. They anticipate an escape from their hectic lives. They want to leave responsibilities, troubles, and stress at the door. The last thing they expect when they ring the doorbell is a grumpy, preoccupied innkeeper. Innkeepers provide more than clean, esthetically appealing lodging, personal service, and food. They offer enchantment.

In *The Re-Enchantment of Every Day Life* Thomas Moore writes, "The soul has an absolute, unforgiving need for regular excursions into enchantment. It requires them like the body needs food and the mind needs thought."

Moore describes enchantment as "a dulling of the mind and a sharpness of perception." One doesn't attain this without taking a time-out from the relentless routine of daily living. Invariably, guests who appeared at breakfast after a restful night's repose did not resemble the ones who had checked in the previous day. The enchantment of a bed and breakfast was often visibly transforming.

Fortunately, our first bed and breakfast stay was so enchanting and transforming in every way that it set the standard for all that followed, including our own. Filled with anticipation and eagerness for our first experience at an inn, I had abandoned thoughts of my daily commutes between two schools and the endless domestic chores that usually awaited me on the weekend. Our destination was located in an older neighborhood of mature trees and attractive, two-story, turn-of-the-century homes. To the background of softly playing classical music, the hostess greeted us with genuine interest and friendliness,

Like the common areas on the ground level, our room, "The Doctor's Retreat," was very serene and simply, but adequately, furnished. My gaze was drawn to the canopy bed in this sunlit room with off-white walls and an original oak floor. A large clawfoot tub and pedestal sink interrupted the flow of the vintage, white, mosaic, floor tiles in the large bathroom. Adjacent was the sun porch where our hostess served an artfully plated breakfast entrée:

freshly squeezed orange juice, French toast made with artisan bread, crisp bacon strips, and whole strawberries nestled in the curve of a muskmelon slice.

Something very transformative occurred that weekend. In the ensuing years, although we experienced other comparable retreats, some more beautiful and grandiose, that first one held its own special place. Much of what we wanted to emulate in our own inn found its roots in that restorative setting.

Enchantment is channeled in many ways. While the innkeeper is a crucial component, there are other avenues for the rejuvenation of guests' spirits. The most obvious one is the visual impact of one's surroundings. This is what some designers call "eye candy."

Casting its spell was Dempster Woods, our two-story, red, brick Italianate. Its porch columns, overhanging eaves, and ornate brackets, painted in red rebellion, cloudy amber, and vogue green, issued an invitation to "wonderland." Floral carpet, an antique German sideboard, stained glass, and textured wallpaper transported our guests into the Victorian era.

One of the home's most spectacular features, although not original, was the varied intricacy of old, tin ceilings, some salvaged from an area church. Before our move to the basement, I had often lain in bed either gazing out the window at the elaborate brackets under the eaves or at the tin ceiling's center and border designs, so painstakingly installed, so lovingly finished by various owners.

In an enchanted place, one is surrounded by authentically individual furnishings, not reproductions. One way we achieved this was to find ways to use what we already had. Ken collects objects which speak to his soul. His ingenuity and handiness transform incomplete, imperfect, old pieces into original masterpieces. With the inversion of an ornate, antique organ header mounted on a wall, we had a period-appropriate shelf for special photos and figurines. An oak, mission-style buffet, minus its mirrored top, acquired new life with the addition of an oak picture frame, fitted with two amber, leaded-glass windows. This buffet stood in front of bay windows in our dining room, where sunlight infused the glass with a golden glow. Voila! This creative combination had brought enchantment. Guests sometimes asked about the uniqueness of this serviceable piece, a magical union of orphans from Ken's collection.

In the kitchen an old cupboard filled one wall and rose to within a foot of the tin ceiling. It was equipped with a bin and a zinc, pull-out, work counter. Many imperfections hinted at its uses in Ken's great-grandparents' farmhouse. Guests often were fascinated with this massive piece. They were astonished to learn that it was one solid unit, which Ken and two of our sons had tipped to a horizontal position and carried into the house. Another piece of interest was an elegant, old, coal stove from the same farmhouse. It provided winter warmth and year-round atmosphere in our enclosed porch.

I am a passionate recycler and garage sale girl. There is immense satisfaction in the re-creation of what I call "déjà vu décor." Homemade quilts graced beds and walls. Some showcased vintage fabric blocks purchased at garage sales. The transformation of two dresses into one eye-catching lap quilt was great fun! My sewing projects are not limited to machine sewing. Hand quilting and embroidery are also very therapeutic. Counted cross stitch samplers appeared in our home in places appropriate to the stitched messages.

The recycling of my grandmother's ivory, brocade drapes into throw pillows, embellished with tassels, tatting, and lace, was another unique element in our home. Gold drapery tassels, glass chandelier pendants, wedding favors, silk corsages, and counted cross stitch Christmas card inserts, made by Ken's aunt, adorned Christmas trees at holiday time. Grandma's hats hung from hooks and perched on closet shelves. Memories of special people and special events appeared everywhere.

Entry into our bed and breakfast engaged other senses. The subtle sounds of Debussy filled the background of the meetings and greetings between guests and hosts. Alluring scents floated in the air: "Smell of Spring" refreshing oil in the foyer, a cappuccino-scented candle burning in the dining room, the wafting aroma of freshly baked, apple-cinnamon muffins in the kitchen. The guestrooms, however, were devoid of all scents in consideration of sensitive, allergy-prone guests.

Since our home's exterior walls were three-bricks thick, the occasional traffic noises were muted. However, the neighborhood abounded with the sounds of nature and of silence. After a night in our inn, city dwellers noted how quiet it was, how well they had slept. The background noise of God's creatures chased away the usual nighttime cares and concerns. Squirrels scurried across the rooftop on a mission to gather acorns and black walnuts.

Robins, blue jays, and cardinals chanted back and forth and flitted from tree to tree. Somewhere in the darkened woods, an owl hooted. As our guests slept, a voiceless, grinning gargoyle, atop a stone pillar, guarded the entrance to the northern half of our two-acre property: a descending, wooded melee of wild raspberry bushes, evergreen, pine, mulberry, and elm trees.

In the sunlit hours, bunnies bounced around in both the domesticated and woodsy areas of our outdoor domain. Butterflies flitted in the flower gardens. On rare occasions a fox, deer, possum, or woodchuck emerged from our own little "Garden of Eden."

From the heavy, ornate oak frame in the parlor, Dan and Elisabeth Lefever, Ken's great-grandparents, silently surveyed the sights, scents, and sounds of our dwelling and its surroundings. Hopefully, they approved of the use of some of their furnishings and our attempt to capture a simpler time, a slower pace, an aura of enchantment.

*   *   *   *   *   *

"I am always relaxed and refreshed when I leave. You are such kind people." **Lincoln, Nebraska**

"Thanks for providing such a wonderful, healing environment." **California**

"Thank you for your gifts of peace and calm in a lovely home you so generously share. You've made our stay a high point of our 16th anniversary." **Anonymous**

"How wonderful to find such an exceptional spot when we so needed to find kindness and wonderful consideration." **Kingsport, Tennessee**

"This was just the break I was needing from 'life.' It was very relaxing, comfortable, and restful." **Hutchinson, Kansas**

"What a nice getaway from the fast pace world of Florida--I felt very at home the minute I walked in the door." **Florida**

8. The "Ins" and "Outs" of Innkeeping

When we were guests instead of hosts, it was usually a positive experience. However, a few inns disappointed us, especially those we visited after we had become innkeepers ourselves. We made comparisons, learned from them, and elevated our expectations.

One holiday weekend in a tourist town, when decent, reasonably-priced lodging was scarce, we rather desperately attempted to book a room where the innkeeper seemed surprisingly uncertain about availability. Some minutes later when we called again, she agreed to offer us lodging. We drove to the inn to survey the situation before confirming our reservation.

We followed her upstairs to see the rooms. I attempted conversation.

"Does anyone help you with the innkeeping?"

"The cat," she replied as one scampered up the steps.

"The Twilight Zone" theme song played in my head.

She continued, "My son comes sometime. Do you ever have a child come to stay with you and they won't leave?"

As I searched for a reply, we moved from room to room and noticed a couple less than reassuring signs. A man's undershirt hung from the sink in the private bathroom, and a discarded, wine bottle foil lay on the floor in front of a fireplace. There were three rooms. Two shared a bath and one had a private bath. I wished to avoid the undershirt bathroom, but I did not want to share a bath.

"Will there be other guests staying tonight?"

"I'm not sure," she answered.

This was not what we had wanted to hear, but since we needed lodging and had run out of other options, we took the room.

A beautiful view of the lake from our small balcony did not dispel my uneasiness.

"Can we push this chest against the door?" I asked Ken before we climbed into bed.

This was the first time I had ever felt uneasy in an inn. The innkeeper's demeanor had not inspired confidence in our choice.

In the morning we were still alive and possessed all of our body parts. The stunning panorama from the balcony dispelled some of our misgivings. However, breakfast was a barely edible disappointment: a dried out scone, several spears of chives draped across a boiled egg, and some sausage. We approached it with as much enthusiasm as she had probably experienced when she prepared it. At least the fare was consistent with the lodgings. We wondered if innkeeping had lost its luster for her.

Other innkeepers, however, overflowed with enthusiasm. It is the custom of some to offer a happy hour during which hors d'oeuvres and beverages are served. After we checked into a very intriguing, historic hotel with its own extensive gift shop on the Mississippi River, we eagerly entered the parlor for "happy hour." We soon discovered that we were captives of the host, who spent the entire hour in detailed narration, with photos, of the massive renovation projects the inn had undergone. "Happy hour" only half lived up to its name. It lasted an hour, but it wasn't happy. The other unique feature of this lodging was the location of the bathroom facilities within each bedroom, including the toilet! A unique interpretation of the open concept!

Artificial enthusiasm was another form of welcome we encountered at a Louisiana inn. "Happy hour" consisted of mint juleps and a pastry treat. The shabby chic charm of a converted "garçonnière," an outbuilding where Cajun male children used to sleep, was unique and comfortable. The innkeepers, who had run a restaurant for years, seemed intent on mechanically moving people in and out of their inn without any personal interaction. We discovered that someone had cleaned our room while we were at breakfast, before we had packed and vacated it. The innkeepers were business execs, who apparently regarded us as dollar signs.

While we did not offer a "happy hour" to our guests, hopefully they had many happy hours. We made an effort to ensure a pleasant stay by being genuinely interested in what they had to say. This meant we took care to facilitate breakfast conversation, not dominate it with house history, family stories, personal travels. If guests asked about these topics, we were more than happy to oblige. On the other hand, if one guest seemed destined to speak endlessly on a topic that held little interest for anyone else, we tried to tactfully steer the conversation to another subject. It was also easily apparent that some guests preferred to talk among themselves and had no desire to chat with us while we served them.

Another formative experience in our growth as innkeepers was a stay at a themed inn. This eastern Missouri inn displayed medical instruments used by Union doctors during the Civil War. The innkeeper, dressed in a military uniform, prepared and served our breakfast. He had once appeared in *The Blue and the Gray,* a public television program of a Civil War re-enactment. As he served us, he demonstrated his proficiency in speaking with different accents. This experience confirmed our plans to include the history of our home and of Ken's French ancestry in what we offered.

More enlightenment occurred when we lodged at a 1950s era motel in a small town in Cajun country. There we ate our first boudin sausages for breakfast and were treated to gumbo and a crawfish boil in the evening. Although the budget-priced, 50s décor room had only basic amenities, the innkeepers were disarmingly personable and eager to enlighten us on the colorful aspects of their Cajun culture.

If we had to choose between a well-appointed establishment and friendly, engaging hosts, we would opt for the latter. We have often experienced both at the same inn. An inn that meets these criteria will open its doors to us on a regular basis. We returned to one such special place multiple times to reconnect with innkeepers who never failed to amaze and entertain us. Their attention to detail and ability to make guests feel like friends refreshed and inspired us.

Every inn takes on the persona of its owners. Whatever the theme, the age, or the setting of the inn, it is ultimately the hosts' talents and hospitality that engender enchantment. The enchantment that refreshes souls.

*   *   *   *   *   *

"Super place, cozy on this early winter day. Great food with just the right amount of hosting." **Dallas, Texas**

"You're a Godsend (in the snow!)" **Yankton, South Dakota**

"How very kind of you to accept us in our plight! We were so grateful to find refuge at your beautiful bed and breakfast. Thank you!" **Lincoln, Nebraska**

9. Innkeeping 101

If a beginner's course on innkeeping was ever offered, we must have been out of the country at the time. A comment we heard quite frequently was, "I've always thought it would be fun to run a bed and breakfast." Never once, until we bought our home, did we entertain such thoughts of "fun." We knew some innkeepers who purchased a house with the plan to renovate it and establish an inn. They interviewed other innkeepers, researched and tried recipes, and basically turned over every stone before they opened their doors. They had taken decisive steps to prepare themselves. What a novel idea!

Our only formal preparation for this new life was to join the state association and follow their suggestions before they inspected and accepted us. It was a fairly simple process (except for pleasing the fire inspector). It was certainly nothing like the preparation a teacher must undergo before taking command of a classroom. We were never "student innkeepers."

While Ken is generally more confident in his decision-making, I am more impulsive. I may struggle with which color to paint a room, but don't hesitate regarding bigger decisions, like buying a house. Somehow we moved forward together without questioning the wisdom of welcoming strangers into our home.

How was this possible? Ken is a farmer and therefore lives a life of risk-taking every day. He embraces adventurous experiences and sometimes has to convince me to share them. While I am leery of first attempts at physically challenging activities such as skiing, I welcome opportunities to grow intellectually and psychologically, like learning a new foreign language or leading a Bible study. Something about the student/ teacher aptitude in me.

Goethe, Germany's equivalent to Shakespeare, said, "Whatever you can do or dream you can, begin it. Boldness has genius, power, and magic to it." Put more simply, "Stretch one's comfort zone."

As an educator I have taken some bold steps in life, some self-imposed, others imposed upon me. One such step was uniting with other parents to form a parent support group which would promote a healthy, safe environment for teens. An outgrowth of this undertaking was, with students' help, the initiation of the first alcohol-free post prom party in our area.

While passionate commitment to this type of project drove me, I faced some daunting professional challenges in other areas. I have always believed that I could do anything if I tried hard enough. One August, two weeks before the opening day of school, I discovered that I was assigned to teach accounting. I pinched myself in an attempt to awaken from this nightmare. Shouldn't my administrator have asked me first about my business background before he made this decision? Ken, who had a business minor, laughed at my predicament. While I have an affinity for language, my vocabulary and aptitude for anything remotely connected to bookkeeping is minus zero. (Is there such a number?)

I naively approached this assignment. I have always believed anything is possible. I just had to stay one step ahead of the students or, at the very least, keep up with them. My brain hurt. During the preparation of each lesson, the only consistent by-products were tears and a headache. When I could no longer help the students, I admitted that I had stretched my comfort zone as far as I could. Fortunately, bad news travels fast in small places. The sixth-grade teacher learned of my dilemma and offered to teach accounting if I would teach English to his students. A no-brainer. I remain eternally grateful!

Several years later the two school districts of my employment changed their foreign language offering from French to Spanish. I began to teach in another area in which I had no official background. I was hopeful for a happier outcome. Since Spanish is similar to French, it was not an impossible stretch to accomplish this; however, two summer months of intense, independent study provided no conversational skills. It was an extremely uncomfortable feeling to have some knowledge of Spanish grammar and vocabulary, but no language facility. By the time I retired nine years later, I had been in a comfortable place in the Spanish classroom for some time.

Innkeeping, on the other hand, was totally unfamiliar territory for both of us. Very seldom did we even have company! We learned to be innkeepers in the same manner that I had learned Spanish. We practiced on the job. Of course, we applied some skills gained through life experience. Ken was a quick learner of setting a proper table, and domestic chores were not foreign to me. Our teaching and farming backgrounds had developed and fine-tuned our coping skills.

An example of our ability to adapt to new situations occurred near the end of a seven-hour return trip from our vacation home. Our farmer son called us with a problem. He and his toddler sons were making a flying trip home from another town because he had received word that his cows were out. He arrived at the farm before we did. We drove straight to the farm without a stop at home to unload the cooler. Our grandsons, strapped in their car seats with the car running, were watching a video while "Daddy" chased cattle. We were there to liberate them and put them to bed.

A farm couple learns to live with day to day unpredictability. Farm families take instant vacations when it rains. When one has dressed for an evening out, the cows have opted for a night out too. A farm wife dutifully drops her current task, even watching a cake bake, when the farmer calls and needs help. "Can you give me a ride?" Lunch is on demand. A farmer sometimes makes the request to eat lunch early. When he's late for a meal and asks what's on the menu, the reply is "Leftovers." And the most frustrating of all is the last minute phone call, "I've already eaten. They provided lunch at the elevator." To this the chef sometimes replies, "You know, I don't cook for pleasure."

Guests didn't usually ask any of these questions, and I certainly didn't offer snotty replies. Nor did I snap at guests who arrived at 8:00 in the evening, interrupting our dinner. Like farming, running an inn involved long days with early beginnings and late endings. Patience was essential. Being late for breakfast didn't exactly endear a guest to a temperamental chef. Neither did a lovingly prepared entrée left on a guest's plate. I hated waste and didn't recycle other people's food. Above all, the theft of a piece of the guests' bacon before it was plated was a capital crime! (The thief was not a paying guest, by the way.) I had to make more bacon and burned the first replacement!

Like farming and teaching, innkeeping demanded adaptability and ingenuity if one wished to do it well. At 11:00 one evening after we had gone to our basement hideout, the doorbell rang. We had informed our guests to ring the doorbell to access us if they needed anything. Our guest's baby needed baby Tylenol. Did I have any? When I replied that I didn't, the desperate mom asked if any place was open where she could buy some. Hitting another dead end, she then asked if we had any rum. I offered her whiskey to rub on the baby's gums, to which she exclaimed, "Nothing like waking you up to ask for liquor for our baby, huh?" Indeed! Whatever occurred, we wore our hospitable faces and tried to meet all requests.

There were times when it was difficult to grin and bear the consequences of thoughtless guests. We missed a wedding ceremony because we waited for the arrival of guests who never materialized. In another instance guests who arrived after we had gone to bed phoned us from their car to tell us that they had left because another person's things were in their room. Apparently, there was some misunderstanding between us regarding which room they had booked. As they drove off into the dark night, I politely and apologetically promised to refund their deposit. Check-in at a reasonable hour was always the best option. It left nothing to chance.

Fortunately, the challenging experiences of innkeeping were infrequent and didn't dim our passion for the profession. We soon learned that being happy innkeepers involved having a quickly accessible sense of humor, the patience of Mother Teresa, the flexibility of an Olympic gymnast, and a willingness to sacrifice one's private life when the doorbell rang. If summoning all of these attributes was difficult at times, we hoped that reasonably good acting convinced our guests that we loved serving all their needs.

*   *   *   *   *   *

"From one B & B owner to another, you have excelled in offering your beautiful home to others." **Dos Cabezas Spirit & Nature Retreat, Arizona**

This seems to be the appropriate place to include a letter from guests who stayed with us regularly in the early years. Their suggestions and positive input reassured us and enabled us to improve our innkeeping day by day, guest by guest.

> We want to thank you very much for our pleasant stay at Dempster Woods a few days ago. Everything was very enjoyable. Yours was our forty-ninth B & B scattered over 12 states and twelfth in Nebraska. We are always concerned that most visitors to B & Bs do not take the time to appreciate all the effort and cost that has gone into the development and maintenance of a fine B & B. As I mentioned, we have developed a rating system which helps

us when recommending B & Bs to our friends. In the rating process we go over our stay and try to identify the strong points of a given B & B. It occurs to me that sharing these lists with our hosts and hostesses might be a good way of showing them our appreciation of their efforts. So I am sending you our list for your use. I should say that our analysis gave Dempster Woods our highest rating, 5*, achieved by only two other Nebraska B & Bs and only ten out of the other 49. Thank you so very much! **Lincoln, Nebraska**

10. Things My "Mothers" Tried to Teach Me

I grew up reading books. A visit to the local library was like a trip to Disneyland for me. The first genre I became addicted to was fairy tales: The Red Fairy Book, The Blue Fairy Book, etc. My overactive imagination and love of the creative process allowed me to live in my own little world where time passed and life's cares didn't exist. This might explain why I learned very few practical homemaking tips. One doesn't learn to cook a meal buried in a book in the bedroom or seated at the piano playing sonatas. The only kitchen activities I recall as a growing girl were peeling potatoes or making a tossed salad.

My mother, who was raised by her grandparents, always told me that she was never allowed to do things in her grandmother's kitchen because the mess was unwelcome. I expect that was also why she never recruited me for many kitchen chores. I am certain that a bookworm apprentice's humble help wouldn't have measured up to her scrutiny. On the other hand, she must have surmised that a bookworm couldn't do too much damage dusting the furniture, the last priority on my household chore list today. I also routinely ironed dad's shirts without supervision.

Ultimately, in my opinion, I entered marriage and adulthood as a true novice and a virgin homemaker. (There is more than one way to be a virgin.) My husband was my guinea pig. It was not until after more than forty years of marriage that he divulged to someone else in my presence that the first meal I had ever cooked for him had made him ill. (That's how I learn most things, when he announces them to someone else!)

Apparently, I fried some hamburgers for the first time the night before his debut as a classroom teacher. He claimed that they were as hard as rocks. He had to call in sick the first day of his new career. Since we were not yet married, I was unaware of this secret until forty years later. Since he had so bravely tolerated my culinary experimentation without complaint, he had my permission to tell guests this story when they commented on the deliciousness of a breakfast entrée.

Like my mother, once I had fine-tuned my cooking skills, my sons occasionally heard me say, "Taste this. It needs something."

Usually, the standard reply was, "It tastes good to me. I can never make it as good as you do."

My feelings exactly. I always thought my rendition of my mother's recipes didn't live up to her standards.

Most women are delighted when hubby suggests eating out. I fit that description until I take the first bite of a truly unremarkable restaurant meal. Although not every dish I prepare is to die for or to die from, I feel betrayed when we have to pay for something extraordinarily ordinary.

To Ken's relief I evolved into a decent cook without being an understudy in my mother's kitchen. Practice, practice, practice.

This illustrates something Benjamin Franklin once said: "Tell me and I forget; teach me and I remember; involve me and I understand."

I understood that I needed to continue to take risks in the kitchen in order to improve. Obviously, culinary progress didn't take place without the added ingredient of humility when the experiment failed.

Humility: an attribute which keeps an innkeeper's life grounded. Mother-in-law: a person who keeps a daughter-in-law humble. If I hadn't had enough lessons in humility cooking for Ken, his mother could have made up the difference in a variety of ways.

One day while we were sitting in our dining room, Ken's mother looked up at the pull-down light fixture above the table and pointed out my lack of housekeeping.

"What's that slice of cheese doing up there?"

How does one answer a question like that? As a mother of three young children, I resolved that day to always check for cheese on the light fixtures.

Every woman knows that a mother can say certain things to a daughter that a mother-in-law should never say. Why did you paint this room that color? Why don't you hire someone to clean your house? If it were me, I wouldn't do it that way, but what do I know? There is no safe reply to these questions when posed by your husband's mother. I took refuge in a humble plea of ignorance or simple silence.

Likewise, when a guest noticed defective innkeeping, it seemed best not to overreact. The most effective one-word acknowledgment I could think of was "Oops!" This is exactly what I said when a guest discovered ants in the sugar bowl on the table in the sun porch.

A big apologetic "Oops" was absolutely necessary when I answered a cell phone call from guests at our facility. We were on our way home from the state track meet in Omaha and had not even seen these guests. They had checked themselves in and spent the first night at the inn without us being there. They wanted to pay their bill and leave one night early because the air conditioner had not worked all night. After that humbling phone call, we resolved to check the air conditioner yearly before the onset of hot weather.

There was one request that always stunned me: permission to print out boarding passes on Ken's printer. This reasonable request revealed the harsh reality that the innkeeper's personal spaces could never pass the white glove test. In fact, location of the computer and the printer on his desk was an adventure in itself. And this task occurred after the shock of passing through the creative clutter of my sewing room and the laundry/mud room to reach the office. A logical person would surmise that I started to tidy up these areas routinely to avoid another ultimate humiliation. This did not happen. There were only so many hours in the day, and I had never liked housecleaning.

Another example of my lack of thoroughness occurred when sister comediennes, yearly guests in our inn, asked me in their uniquely humorous way if I knew there was clothing in a dresser drawer in their room. They described the clothing in enough detail that I was able to identify who had left it there long, long ago. I made a mental note to remember to routinely check the drawers after guests departed.

A more public humiliation confronted me one morning as we chatted with our week-long guests around the table after breakfast.

Their four-year-old daughter came downstairs exclaiming, "Oh, Sandy, you are going to be so pwoud of me."

She showed me her handful of dead lady bugs that she had retrieved from under the beds in "Alice's Window on the Woods." This was the most popular hangout for the bugs' annual invasion during the autumn months when they abandoned the outdoors for warmer surroundings. In my defense, even a daily vacuuming didn't eliminate every trace of their residency. However, it was obvious that I had succeeded in ignoring these little critters for quite some time.

A few minutes later, this adorable child appeared again at the table, holding a snake skin entirely too near me.

"Yikes," I screamed and nearly knocked over my chair.

"Oh, Sandy, that was so funny!"

I was silently grateful that she had found this wonder of nature outdoors, not in the house.

Humble pie! Not my favorite dessert. Thanks to my mother-in-law, I had learned to swallow my pride, bite my tongue, and become capable of weathering the moments when all was not perfect in the inn. Thanks to my mom for providing me with a good role model. In spite of her own lack of preparation while growing up, she had become a quality homemaker. I think there is still hope for me.

*   *   *   *   *   *

"You are such gracious hosts! Because my parents are gone, we can no longer come back to their home, and it is nice to have a 'new' place that we can think of as 'home.' We enjoy very much your artistic touches throughout the house. You have a great talent for making the rooms appear tasteful as well as 'homey.'" **South Pasadena, California**

"When I arrived a week ago I was exhausted and in need of a well-deserved vacation. I thoroughly enjoyed my visit to Nebraska and your grand hospitality. It was just the right place for me." **Rockford, Illinois**

11. The Innkeeper Is "Out to Lunch"

As is already evident, some of our guests have had a few good laughs at my expense. Behind the closed doors of their rooms, they have probably even expressed genuine concern for my mental well-being.

When I answered the doorbell to guests one fall afternoon, a Chinese pug also greeted me.

Of a generally non-assertive nature, I steeled myself to inform them that dogs were not allowed in the house.

Before I opened my mouth with the unwelcome news, the gentleman smiled and asked, "Is this your dog?"

"No, I don't know whose dog it is, but my son has one just like it."

It took me some long seconds to realize that it *was* our son's dog. I had forgotten that he had come to help harvest and had left Lucy with me at the house.

I could probably easily justify this mindlessness by citing how many hats I wore in a day's time. An autumn day could look like this:

Arise early to prepare breakfast
Visit with guests
Do the dishes
Empty wastebaskets and tidy guests' rooms and bathrooms
Apply makeup and change clothes for work
Prepare lunches and deliver them to the harvesters
Drive twenty minutes to my school
Teach four different preparations
Purchase breakfast and lunch supplies for the next day
Leave a note and a house key for new guests
Walk two miles while watching for guests' arrival
Help harvesters move to a different field
Keep the grandchildren during their mom's exercise class
Prepare dinner and do the dishes
Set the table and do some prep work for breakfast
Practice hymns for church

In addition to these duties, there was the seasonal task of mowing an acre of grass and maintaining entirely too many flowerbeds. Guests sometimes found me pulling weeds in my work clothes and floppy hat. Of course, autumn follows summer, and leaves fall from trees. My misguided propensity to haul bundles of raked leaves to the woods resulted in many visits to the chiropractor and physical therapist. I completely understood why the innkeeper at a certain establishment appeared at breakfast in wrinkled clothing with bags under her eyes.

Unfortunately, I can't even convince myself that too many hats cause my brain to malfunction. The ultimate truth is that I have functioned this way much of my life, or at least since I uttered the fateful words "I do!" Before children arrived, my husband, in humorous frustration, exclaimed, "If you dyed your hair blonde, you'd be a dumb blonde!" I've never managed to shed that label. No offense to blonds intended! Apparently, they are getting an undeserved reputation. I am a brunette.

The first time my significant unawareness became painfully obvious was when I stopped to admire the bathroom walls I had just finished papering. I discovered I had mismatched all the seams! The seams of gracefully ascending vertical rows of seaweed and snails converged to create a row of two-eyed sea creatures who stared back at me. I had butted together two different snails which appeared as mismatched eyes. They mocked me every time I sat on the porcelain throne, a burden I bore until we moved to a different house.

Cars also challenge my awareness. One day as Ken pulled into our driveway with me in the passenger seat, I noticed my copper-colored Lincoln Continental wasn't in the driveway.

"I wonder where my car is. I guess Nate must have taken it."

"You're in it," was Ken's reply. (I know. That's hard to believe.)

I have also had a particularly difficult time switching back and forth between vehicles. In my "zone" I reach for the gear shift and turn on the windshield wipers. I fumble around trying to find the door unlock button. Car color calls to me. I automatically head for a gray car without noticing that there are four gray cars in the vicinity. Although I have climbed into the wrong car several times, awareness of my surroundings remains a weak point.

Another car tale. One mid-May day another teacher accompanied me to student graduation parties. Routinely, I removed my fitover sunglasses each time we stopped at a party and put them on again when we returned to the car. It was dark when we left the last of ten parties, many miles from town. I turned on the headlights and commented on how odd the oncoming headlights looked.

"I don't think my headlights are working right," I repeated several times.

Finally, after several miles my colleague very tactfully asked, "I don't want to offend you, but do you usually wear sunglasses when you drive at night?"

Most people expect teachers to be responsible, focused individuals. Yet, I was living proof that there are momentary exceptions to this ideal. One time during parent/teacher conferences, the school office paged me for a phone call from the local restaurant. As I picked up the phone, I suddenly realized that I had left without paying for my meal!

So, is it any wonder that after our guests had finished their breakfast, I realized that I had forgotten to serve the bacon, which was still in the microwave for a little warm-up? A sense of humor is wonderfully redeeming. I plopped the serving plate full of bacon on the table and announced, "Here's dessert."

Breakfast entrées shouldn't require too many instructions before the guests dig in. I only forgot one time to demonstrate how to use the new syrup dispenser, which was really intended for honey. The spout was not at the top, but at the bottom of the container. A guest was so startled and embarrassed when she squeezed the lever and tipped the dispenser. The syrup drizzled from the hole in the bottom and landed everywhere but on her crêpes.

At odd moments a light bulb dispels the fogginess in my brain. Hours after our guests had paid their bill and left for a flight out of Omaha, that still, small voice told me to look at my copy of their receipt. A hot flash passed through me. I discovered that instead of adding the lodging and sales taxes to the room charge I had subtracted them. A one hundred dollar deficit. Since it was such a large amount and these guests always stayed with us when they visited local relatives, I called them at the airport to report my error. No wonder I had failed at teaching accounting!

At times I recall the wisdom a high school classmate shared with me as we pondered an array of frozen items in the grocery store, "We're getting to the age when we can hide our own Easter eggs."

Yet, for some strange reason whenever I misplace anything important, I panic. I jump to the wrong conclusion. I am certain that I left my purse at church, that my cell phone fell out of my pocket, or someone took it. This attitude sometimes led me to suspect that a guest had taken something I couldn't find. In one instance I contacted a guest to ask if she had inadvertently forgotten to leave their key to our front door. I also wondered if she knew anything about the hair dryer which was no longer in its place. The answer to both was negative. The key never materialized, but I found the hair dryer in a drawer in the hall linen closet. Then I remembered that I had "hidden" it there myself!

In view of my past history, it was not in character for me to assume the blame for a missing napkin ring. While setting the table, I came up with only eleven of the twelve fleur-de-lis rings. I counted them several times and looked under the table and in the buffet. Number twelve was nowhere to be found. Then, as was my habit, I became suspicious enough to think I knew which one of our guests was the likely culprit.

At breakfast the next morning, I apologized for being short one napkin ring, I emphasized that they had all been there when we had served breakfast the previous day. Later that day the napkin ring mysteriously reappeared on the dining room table. It was reassuring to know that I hadn't absentmindedly put it in an illogical place. I felt empowered to have been right just this once.

In an attempt to justify my occasional mindlessness, I like to give my husband a gentle reminder, "I don't have dementia. I'm just a dumb blonde, remember?"

*   *   *   *   *   *

"Your home is so beautiful and it is so nice you share your gifts and talents in such a caring way. God bless you and your family. This is the day the Lord has made: I will rejoice and be glad in it." **Arizona**

12. The Master of the House

In the early days of sharing our home with strangers, I discovered that I really didn't know my husband as well as I had thought. For years he had very successfully hidden talents I had not known existed. These gifts emerged gradually when the innkeeping business picked up.

A certain routine developed between us as we prepared to serve our guests. I usually arranged the placemats, napkins, tableware, sugar, salt, and pepper on the table the night before. This allowed me to get up a little later and to focus on food preparation in the morning. Ken prepared coffee and juice and filled the water goblets. He filled the coffee carafe with hot water to warm it up before replacing it with his freshly brewed coffee. Where did he learn that? At the sound of creaking stairs and voices, he appeared in a "Prairie Home Companion" souvenir apron, which read "Café Boeuf--Home of the Candlelit Dinner for Two."

While I might be in the kitchen stressing over a not-so-perfect entrée, Ken calmly filled coffee cups, served orange juice, and initiated conversation with our guests. This reticent partner of many years was a master of chitchat! He entertained strangers, asked them about themselves, and answered their questions.

When I plated food, he was at my elbow ready to whisk each plate into the dining room. In an effort to serve everyone quickly, he even began to artfully contribute to the presentation. He dusted crêpes with powdered sugar, twisted orange slices for garnish, added a sprig of mint from the herb garden. Previously, Ken's only contribution to the culinary arts had been making chocolate popcorn on Sunday nights. This special treat should have provided a clue to his latent, culinary creativity.

When guests asked us to join them at the table, a mutual exchange of information often transpired. This was the time to respond to curious guests' queries: what made us decide to open a bed and breakfast, what kind of crops did we grow on our farm, what variety of grapes were planted in our vineyard, what were the sources of employment in Geneva.

Before departure, if needed, Ken provided guests with a map or directions and often, at their requests, acted as photographer. When Mother Nature had deposited some overnight precipitation, Ken was up early to shovel the walk. Occasionally, he scraped a guest's windshield. This was the predictable, familiar Ken. I am still in awe of "kitchen Ken" and "conversational Ken."

Perhaps the most profound affirmation of Ken's prowess in the kitchen came after we had hosted seventeen, stranded motorists during a blizzard. They began appearing at our door mid-afternoon. An employee from the local convenience store sent the first arrivals. When I began to recognize her voice on the phone asking if we had room for more people, I knew we would never be able to accommodate every request.

Ken catered the evening meal for our guests. It consisted of Campbell's soup, sandwiches, and cookies, all purchased at the local grocery store. Some guests retrieved wine from their cars, including a chocolate wine, which they shared. They ate in shifts at the dining room table. They slept in beds, recliners, and on the two futons. A family with young children slept on the parlor floor.

In a lighthearted moment, while the first shift sat at the dining room table, I turned to Ken to propose a toast, "How do you like the surprise party I planned for your birthday?"

The story didn't end there. Over a year later, I answered a phone call from Minnesota, wondering who this could be. Since our personal number was also our business number, we always answered the phone.

"I was one of those guests at your house during the blizzard last winter. I just called to ask you what kind of coffee your husband served. That was the best coffee I've ever had."

I told him I had no idea, that it was probably whatever had been on sale at the time. A tribute to "barista Ken."

While Ken's contributions remained generally consistent, there were those unusual requests, some of which were more labor intensive: moving furniture, converting a king bed to twins to accommodate guests' requests, and the urgent, unpleasant task of unclogging a toilet. Other services he provided, such as farm tours and combine rides, were memorable for guests and innkeeper.

Most husbands don't have strong opinions about furniture choices or placement. Ken is not most husbands. He has raised chinchillas in a bedroom, planted a vineyard, made wine in the basement, processed newly harvested sorghum (which boiled over, seeped through the stove insulation, and ran into the basement).

In a new role as innkeeper, his enterprising mind turned to ideas for outfitting our much larger home. He purchased unique pieces of furniture that captured his interest, such as antique armoires, a massive, carved German sideboard, which covered one wall in our parlor, and a seven-piece, Eastlake parlor set upholstered in gold velvet. Never mind that it was to rest on a floral carpet with shades of pink, mauve, and green! Never mind that when we later sold this home, we couldn't find a buyer for this furniture. (We finally donated it to the Stuhr Museum in Grand Island, Nebraska, where it has found a place in one of their farm homes in their prairie town setting.)

One of his attempts to execute an upgrade resulted in a quirky outcome which plagued us for years. He installed a remote doorbell apparatus so that we could hear its ring on the other floors. He must have gotten his wires crossed. Whenever someone flipped the remote light switch (another upgrade) at the foot of the back stairs, the doorbell rang.

On one occasion when we were asleep, we heard the doorbell. Ken headed up the basement stairs, only to discover that one of our adult children had returned home and flipped the light switch on the way upstairs.

On the other hand, whenever anyone actually rang the doorbell, the upstairs light came on. It kept us mentally active remembering to shut off the light after someone had rung the bell.

One afternoon when we had returned from a trip, I observed, "It looks like someone has rung the doorbell while we were gone."

Our friends' befuddled expressions prompted an explanation: there was a light in the upstairs, hallway window.

Although Ken never attempted to eliminate this confusion, he was usually relentless in his efforts to solve a sticky problem. After a few years of illegally hosting more than three guests simultaneously, he contacted the fire inspector again, hoping to resolve their previous differences. The addition of an outdoor fire escape from a hall window allowed us to accomplish a couple things: the retention of the original transoms above the bedroom doors upstairs, thus preserving historic authenticity, and the operation of our inn within the law.

When the master of the house had set his mind to something, I was happy to sit back and observe him at work. Unlike the thieving innkeeper in Victor Hugo's *Les Miserables*, Ken didn't just claim to be honest. He *was* honest, and, for that reason, I proclaim him to be "the best innkeeper in town."

He greeted weary guests with an offer to carry their luggage upstairs. He was always eager to fulfill every wish, unless they had parked on the lawn or usurped the television remote! The violation of these unposted rules transformed the otherwise mild-mannered Ken into that other innkeeper, Monsieur Thenardier.

*   *   *   *   *   *

"Thank you so much for the wonderful place to stay. We had a great time. Mike will always remember this trip especially finding out Ken was his high school teacher." **Waverly, Nebraska**

"Your attention to the children was greatly appreciated. Kyle loved the visit to the farm and his 'ride' on all the tractors." **Mesa, Arizona**

13. Behind the Scenes

One holiday weekend before we opened "Dempster Woods," Ken and I decided to use our gift certificate to a Nebraska bed and breakfast in a metropolitan setting. We had arrived at the tail end of the holiday, eager to explore the interior of the impressive, spacious, Gothic Revival mansion. We were the only guests after an exceptionally busy weekend.

When our hostess greeted us at breakfast, I noticed how tired she looked. I asked how many rooms there were and if someone helped her and her husband. Her response revealed the reason for her bedraggled appearance. She, her husband, and a niece, when available, cleaned all seven rooms and bathrooms in addition to the performance of the culinary duties. Formerly teachers, they had made a huge investment to take this new career path. I was certain she had been hoping for no guests at the end of this long holiday weekend.

Years later when we found ourselves in the same scenario to a much lesser degree, I recalled the weary innkeeper. I understood completely as we stood on the front steps for a photo by our departing guests. Ken, a creature of habit, had performed his morning toiletries. I, on the other hand, had charged into the day with the most important task in mind, the preparation of the breakfast entrées. Devoid of make-up, I gave my best smile, exposing teeth I hadn't taken the time to brush. Occasionally I had to remind myself that it was not about me. It was about our guests who wanted to end their stay with a photo of the house and their hosts.

Only after we had served the main entrée did I feel like I had reached the moment when I could relinquish the chef apron, appear in the dining room, and finally relate to guests. When I took my foot off the accelerator and my focus from the kitchen, I noticed things I had been oblivious to in the flurry of preparation and an otherwise overly full schedule. Things like smudges on the beveled glass window in the door to the porch (souvenirs of grandchildren), a drapery valance that was out of alignment, dust on the secretary desk.

The work load grew as news of our endeavors at "Dempster Woods" reached the locals. They began to recommend us to their visiting friends and relatives. Groups of people who rented the entire house for several days was the ideal situation. It meant less work and more income.

Soon it became apparent that hiring someone to help would facilitate the process of making four beds and cleaning the bathrooms, especially when there was a quick turnover. Never having enjoyed domestic chores like my mother did, I was appreciative of some additional expertise. Six different cleaning ladies assisted me through the years. They taught me a lot about housekeeping: use of Murphy's Wood Soap for window cleaning, how to assemble bedding with hospital corners, creative techniques for folding towels.

We shared much more than practical housekeeping tips. We made beds and conversation and developed a friendship while we worked. Some of them were in awe of how much work was involved in the innkeeping profession. One of them, a teenager, inspired me with her willingness to help clean after detasseling corn all morning in the summer heat. I appreciated their efforts to assist me on an "as needed" basis from week to week. I admired their energy and capacity for doing a labor-intensive task in a dedicated, thorough fashion. Thanks to them, we always received a five-star rating in the cleanliness category on the guests' comment cards.

So much more than just having fun was involved in this way of life. I always hoped that guests were not able to hear the muttering and self-talk which occurred in the kitchen during our preparation time. The popular opinion that chefs are temperamental holds a grain of truth. From my own experience, however, it was not about a passionate, creative person becoming a chef, but about an amateur chef becoming crazy. We strove to be prepared to handle any contingency without our guests' knowledge. For example, one morning between entrées, Ken removed a tick which was attached to my back.

My initial approach to the culinary aspect of innkeeping was to do what I knew best. I prepared my first dishes from French recipes I had previously tested on my students. In addition, thanks to the graciousness of some innkeepers we had patronized, I expanded my repertoire by using their recipes, some of which I have shared in this book.

I functioned best when I prepared as much as possible in advance. When milk approached its expiration date, I heated the cast iron skillet and made dozens of crêpes. These became our signature entrée, one that I could retrieve from the freezer and fill with whatever I desired. Also in the freezer was homemade bread supplied by two local women at different intervals of our business. I had discovered their talents after purchasing their luscious loaves at community garage sales. The best life had to offer was in our own backyard.

In our attempts to establish a business and continually improve the ambience and the comfort of guests, we held informal family-furniture-moving events without much advance notice. They often started with a casual question, "By the way, could you stop by when you're in town to help Dad move some furniture?" Or something like, "While you're here for a few days, would you and your brother be able to do some heavy lifting?"

Holidays were opportunities for much more than celebrating. One Thanksgiving morning, having become dissatisfied with watching television at the north end of the house far away from guests, we gave our sons the opportunity to provide us with a new relaxing room. They moved the piano from the library into the parlor. We were now comfortable enough in our roles to relax in the library/TV room, closer to guests' comings and goings.

Of course, when Christmas approached, in order to accommodate a large tree in the parlor window, Ken and I carried an antique, oak loveseat up the steep stairs to one of the bedrooms to make room for the tree. We retrieved artificial trees from storage in the basement. Gathering the tree decorations was a two-person project. From an elevated crawl space in the basement Ken shoved each appropriately labeled, storage tub through the opening. I stood on a ladder ready to grab hold of each one. Then I indulged in one of my favorite passions, the decoration of seven trees! The white glow of the trees in the front windows when I returned home at night never failed to fill me with warm serenity and a sense of completeness.

A much more precarious undertaking was moving bathtubs. A supreme, physical challenge was hoisting a super-sized, cast iron, clawfoot tub up the steps of the outdoor basement exit. After the successful accomplishment of this Herculean task, Ken and son deposited it on our lawn. The tub and a pedestal sink remained there for lack of a Part B to the plan. I filled them with wheel barrows of dirt from the vegetable garden and planted geraniums and rose moss. I convinced myself that they appeared to be thoughtfully contrived, eccentric additions to our outdoor property.

An even more life-threatening task was the transportation of a new Jacuzzi tub upstairs to the second floor. The former walk-in closet would become a second bathroom. Without a single swear word, Ken and son painstakingly grunted and groaned their way, step by step, up the narrow, steeply pitched stairs to the top. Manipulation of the tub over the stair banister to make the turn was a tricky endeavor. Eyes cast upward, I prayed at the bottom of the stairs.

It should be pretty obvious that we have always been a couple who tried to do it all, sometimes too much in too little time. It wasn't unusual for me to be hanging pictures on the newly painted, bedroom walls just moments before a group of eleven college students arrived to claim their rooms. It had been somewhat risky to tackle a renovation project between guests. Nor was it a surprise that Ken was still vacuuming while I ironed a skirt when an Arts' Council member arrived to take her station at our house for the community tour of homes.

"Wanna be" innkeepers probably romanticize the profession. It looks easy, interesting, fun! The dream job! The reality was this: guests passed through the door to the soothing serenity of their destination, unaware that moments ago the smiling hosts had just completed a marathon of frantic preparation. At long last, after introductions had taken place, all was well at the inn. Or so it seemed.

*　　　*　　　*　　　*　　　*　　　*

"It was very special to be in Geneva for Dad's 65th GHS reunion, and staying here at Dempster Woods was a real highlight. Your breakfast was delicious, and your home beautiful! Good luck with the winemaking, Ken!"
Orange, California

14. Expect the Unexpected

No matter how well our careers in education and agriculture had prepared us, we weren't, by any means, equipped to tackle all the unforeseen circumstances of innkeeping without encountering surprises and sometimes frustration.

In the early years of this new way of life, I was so anxious for guests that I jumped up expectantly whenever the phone rang. Previously, I had always regarded the telephone as a source of annoyance, interruption, and waste of time. One day as we sat on the porch enjoying a rare, rainy, August downpour, the phone rang. I sprinted into the house, through the parlor and the dining room, to answer it.

"This is the Goldenrod Motel calling. We are full and wondered if you would take a couple people who need lodging."

I happily agreed to accommodate them, and the voice on the other end continued, "Okay. I'll send them over. They're on motorcycles."

Uncertain whether that was a warning or just helpful information, I conjured up images of a couple of edgy-looking, tattooed thugs. With a little apprehension, we waited on the porch for their arrival. That still, small voice again reminded me that these bikers might be angels in disguise.

A male and a female, both obviously senior citizens, got off their bikes. They were on their way to Sturgis, South Dakota, where every August thousands of bikers gathered for the annual Sturgis Motorcycle Rally. The male was a retired Dallas policeman. They actually were "angels," whose mission was biker ministry. I felt chastised that I had jumped to conclusions and relegated all bikers into a single category. Before they left the following morning, Ken and I borrowed their leather jackets and mounted one of the bikes for a photo, which later appeared in our Christmas letter.

Another biker spontaneously appeared on our doorstep one hot, blustery, summer afternoon, when God must have opened the gates of hell to give us a taste of the temperature down there. This windblown, exhausted rider of a pedal bicycle was desperate for a room.

"I will sleep on the floor if I have to. I have ridden 120 miles today from Kansas. I can't go another mile."

The 30ish father of three was extremely relieved to crash at our establishment, in a bed.

Every June avid cyclists and a few adventurous crazies participated in the BRAN (Bike Ride Across Nebraska). The route changed yearly, and this particular year the Geneva community was privileged to be one of the overnight stops. Many bikers had set up pup tents and camped in the designated area while others sought more comfortable lodging. We had been anticipating Senator Chuck Hagel's wife who was riding, but circumstances resulted in a cancellation. A couple middle-aged women aptly replaced her as our entertainment. They kiddingly chided one another about the sanity of their choice to do this "fun" event for the first (and last!) time. The eighty mile ride that day into a biting, hot headwind had not really been that much fun.

Whenever I opened the door to expected guests, it was a surprise to finally meet and greet the persons who had reserved a room. Occasionally, the faces at the door did not match my mental images of the guests. I was sometimes terribly off the mark. When an older man and a younger woman appeared one afternoon, I was certainly very curious. They had come to attend a local wedding. Was this a couple or a father and a daughter? The man in a suit and a baseball cap had a scruffy, gray beard which matched his long locks. His blond partner wore a slinky, black dress and stiletto heels. Evidently, she took personal grooming much more seriously than her companion.

The next morning, seeing no wedding rings, I was still trying to determine this couple's connection. When we inquired about the wedding, the woman proceeded to describe in detail a practical joke she had played on her companion's mother while they helped decorate the reception facility. Proudly, she shared that she had put a basketball under her shirt and told his mother she was pregnant. When his mother reacted as she had hoped, she pulled her shirt up and the ball popped out. To my shock and to Ken's delight, she demonstrated this last part by pulling up her top at the breakfast table. That dispelled any doubt I had about their relationship.

Not all surprises were that entertaining, especially when a female guest complained at breakfast, "There was no hot water for a shower this morning."

Bravely, the gentleman who had rented the room with the Jacuzzi tub announced that he had taken a whirlpool bath that morning. Oops! Since it's really not pleasant for guests to have too many "house rules," we weren't going to add one that prohibited whirlpool baths in the morning. Instead, that one incident resulted in the purchase of a new seventy-five gallon hot water tank.

This tub later became the source of another unwelcome outcome. When I opened the door to clean that bathroom after our Colorado guest had departed, I wondered if a few more rules wouldn't be a good idea after all. I was dismayed to see a residue the color of Colorado clay in the relatively new Jacuzzi. No amount of cleaning product or elbow grease ever removed that rusty color from the recessed part of the jets. I wondered if our guest had soaked in the tub wearing his cowboy boots!

Cleaning rooms in a timely manner assured us of handling the surprise of "drop in" guests. A couple young men rang the doorbell at 8:00 one evening. They wanted a room for about five hours, just enough time to get some sleep before their "rescuer" arrived to haul their trailer back to Kansas. Local law enforcement had stopped them and issued a ticket for driving without a commercial driver's license. Apparently, they had been unaware that they needed one. They were not to leave Geneva for a certain number of hours or pull the trailer home illegally. The commercial driver would arrive at about 1:00 in the morning. The young man was so stressed and grateful that he added a twenty-dollar tip to his payment for the room before he headed upstairs. I read his name in the county courthouse notes in the local paper a few weeks later.

Another unexpected turn of events, which we had hoped to never encounter, occurred only twice. While most people were very agreeable to the few rules we had, some couldn't seem to part with their dogs. To our knowledge there were only two overnight dogs in our establishment. I discovered the first one when I went upstairs to relay some information to our guests. The young man who opened the door was holding a small dog which he promised would sleep in its carrier. I let him keep the dog and didn't charge an additional fee. Naively, I hoped that it would not happen again.

Since I hadn't banished the first dog from the property, I couldn't very well tell "Red Skelton" that he wasn't allowed to bring his dog into the house. "Red" was really an actor who was impersonating Red Skelton in the Geneva Arts Council presentation at the local theater the following day. In fact, he had been a personal friend of Skelton's and was the only person with access to his material and the right to perform it.

The actor was recovering from cancer and chemotherapy treatments. His pet was a medical dog trained to bark if there was too much dust in the environment. Although I kept the guest rooms dust-free, I couldn't remember when I had last dusted the common areas on the main floor. During breakfast I sat on the edge of my chair. I waited for the dog on his lap to bark. It did not! It should be blatantly obvious by now that dusting is not one of my top priorities.

As I have now revealed my number one innkeeper pet peeve (guests who arrive with animals), how uncharacteristic of me to allow an entourage of various kinds of animals to spend a couple nights in our home! How did this happen?

After our guests had left for the day, I went up the back stairs to empty trash and freshen their quarters. The door of an adjacent bedroom was open, and, to my amazement, it was occupied by a bed full of little critters, stuffed, that is. Dozens of them. Of every variety. Unbelievable! The next morning I couldn't resist asking them about their "pets."

Without blinking an eye, the wife matter-of-factly replied, "Oh, they travel everywhere with us. They have their own special suitcase."

Her husband added, also very matter-of-factly, "They even sat with us in a circle around a campfire at Mackinac Island in Michigan."

A very rare event occurred at that moment. I was at a loss for words.

Although we did not mind the stuffed animal lovers bedding their critters in a room they had not reserved, we never expected guests to enter the private areas of our home. One morning when I emerged from the basement to prepare breakfast, I nearly collided with two unfamiliar young men in the back hallway beyond the kitchen. They were wandering around in the part of the house which was off limits to guests. Apparently, they had dropped in to see some of our guests. It didn't take long for me to hang a sign labeled "Private" on the door which separated that part of the house from the rest. Would a sign on the swinging door effectively ensure our privacy?

Behind that door was our personal bathroom, my sewing room, the laundry room, and Ken's office, all of which did not meet the Nebraska Association of Bed and Breakfast standards. After breakfast more than a few guests asked, "Is there a bathroom I can use down here?" or "Can I have access to a computer to print boarding passes?" I wanted to reply, "Absolutely not!" Although Ken always graciously allowed them to use his office, I lied about there being a bathroom.

Of course, guests and potential guests asked a lot of questions. We usually knew how to answer unexpected queries, but occasionally one caught us unprepared. One such quirky inquiry occurred when Ken answered the phone. The caller wanted to know if we rented rooms during the day and if he could see the room. Ken agreed to this and was waiting on the front porch, brimming with curiosity. Much to his disappointment, the only arrivals were some school colleagues and I with our sack lunches. We spent our lunch hour speculating on the possible reasons for renting a room during the day. In addition to the obvious ones, we innovative educators conjured up a few others which I will not mention here.

Many guests asked the most predictable question, "What made you decide to run a bed and breakfast?" We always both replied, almost in unison, "We're crazy, I guess."

The most thought-provoking question anyone had ever asked was, "What do you do for fun around here?"

Without hesitation Ken replied, "Run a bed and breakfast." I agreed.

*   *   *   *   *   *

"Thanks so much for letting us stay here so unexpectedly and when we needed it so much. We very much appreciate your hospitality. Thanks for everything you did for my family three weeks ago!" **Columbia, Missouri**

"Thanks for not turning us away when we showed up on your door step! What a treasure you have here. God bless you!" **Alva, Oklahoma**

"We had to come back to our hometown in our 50s to meet two wonderful people we should have known better years ago! We thank you so very much for your incredible hospitality, your kindness and graciousness to our extended family. It made what was a sad occasion a little easier to bear." **Whidbey Island, Washington**

15. Do unto Others

Wilbur and Marge ambled into the dining room. About midway through strawberry crêpes, Marge piped up, "You wouldn't want to sell those hats upstairs?"

"Hats?"

My slow brain waves tried to process this request before she replied. She and Wilbur weren't staying in the room with the old hats in the drawers. She had been snooping in the other rooms!

"Oh, no!" I replied as politely as I could. "They belonged to my grandmother. I discovered them in her cedar chest which my dad gave us."

"It never hurts to ask," she countered. "By the way, we couldn't find the kitchen light switch last night. I tried to make a cup of tea in the microwave in the dark, and sparks flew," she added.

That explained the gold-rimmed Gevalia coffee cup sitting on the kitchen counter. I imagined Marge stumbling around in the dark kitchen as she fumbled for coffee cups in the cabinets and filled one with water. The light switch wasn't even in the kitchen, but in the hall behind the stove wall. I wondered if she had flipped on the wall switch just inside the kitchen door. The grinding of the garbage disposal in the dark of night would startle even the most adventurous guests.

It made me think about how much else she may have discovered in her nocturnal meanderings. Since we lived in our inn and the kitchen was our family kitchen, we did not offer amenities such as self-made tea-at-any-time. This was the first time that we were aware of guests feeling that much at home.

Our conversation with Marge and Wilbur moved on to other topics and ended with a discussion of how the temperature had dropped fifteen degrees overnight. Marge lamented that she had no jacket because she had left hers at her sister's home the day before. Bless my generous husband's heart. He left the room and returned with a hunter green, hooded jacket for Marge to wear.

"Oh, no!" she protested. "I can manage. I don't want to take your jacket."

"Why doesn't Ken offer to sell it to her?" I thought sarcastically. She was willing to buy Grandma's hats.

Kind soul that he is, he replied with an encouraging grin, "You don't know how many of those jackets a farmer has! Please take it. I won't miss it."

Marge and Wilbur were very grateful. As was I. Grateful that they were leaving, grateful that Ken is always so gracious and tactful, grateful that I had kept my inhospitable thoughts to myself.

Although we had been happy to provide the warmth of Ken's jacket to a guest, we used some restraint in mailing items to guests who had left something behind at our inn. This is one of the ten commandments of innkeeping: **"Thou shall not return an item unless a guest has called and requested it."** A naïve, trusting soul, I was unaware of the need for such a business practice in the early years of hosting guests. Hopefully, whoever had received a shipment of used underwear or a lady's nightgown recognized the item I had mailed to them.

Through the years, when the situation seemed straightforward enough, we returned books, earrings, and clothing via parcel post. When I discovered a man's suit left behind in an armoire, Ken delivered it to his car in front of a local church during the service. A bag of ladies' shoes went on a road trip with us. Their owner met us in a small Missouri town which was on the way to our destination. We sometimes left parcels on our front porch for area residents to pick up and return to relatives who had stayed with us.

In spite of all these efforts, we still garnered a collection of unclaimed items: a baseball, disposable diapers, a bar of soap between the sheets (restless leg syndrome?), children's toys, a tube of lipstick, shampoo, bath gel, a pillow, a voltage converter, women's flip-flops, a drawer full of men's, women's and children's clothing. Fortunately, the guests who subsequently stayed in that room and opened the drawer were yearly returnees. Whoops! This was what my cleaning lady called "selective cleaning." I didn't have to call Sherlock Holmes to unravel the mystery of that assortment of clothing. I knew who had left it, and they had apparently never missed it.

One day when I entered a guest room to strip the bed, I spotted the most shocking item ever left behind. A black, more than gently used, men's thong hung from the knob of a Victorian chair. I gasped in horror! If Senator Charles Sloan's ghost had been seated on that chair, it wouldn't have startled me more. I knew it did not belong to our most recent guests. They must have found it somewhere in the room and left it for me to see. I hoped with all my heart that they had not taken a comment card to mail to the state association.

And then, an even more undesirable possibility struck me. What if that thong had been hanging there when I had cleaned the room before the arrival of these guests? I have never been known to have a keen eye for detail. Could that item have escaped my attention in my final inspection? Had I done a final inspection? Another item the post office never handled.

The thong story is one of those anecdotes innkeepers share with one another. Ken and I related this to the hosts of a Des Moines inn as we swapped stories and laughed over a delectable breakfast. We knew that we would return to stay with them because we had made a strong connection. Obviously, the feeling was mutual because they drove four hours for the sole purpose of a one-night stay in our inn. The morning after they left, I discovered a lacy, black, large-sized thong draped over a lampshade in their room with a note which read, "The legend lives on."

Unfortunately, although we tried to continue the thong saga, we were unsuccessful. When we learned that our Russian guests' next overnight stop would be in Des Moines, we encouraged them to stay at our friends' inn, but they had already booked hotel rooms. Sadly, it was not possible to return the thong with a note, "From Russia, with love."

*   *   *   *   *   *

"How we hate to leave!! This has been home away from home. Your many talents and your graciousness will be long remembered." **Round Lake Beach, Illinois**

"Thanks for being such a gracious hostess and being so patient and kind, in being flexible with our circumstances. We pray that God's Kingdom will come soon and that his will be done in heaven and also upon the earth." **Idaho**

"Thanks so much for a really wonderful visit with a "warm" welcome to Nebraska. May our Lord Jesus Christ bless your family with the peace that comes from having a personal relationship with Christ." **Pennsylvania**

16. Making Connections

A bed and breakfast is an optimal choice for a weekend getaway where one can be anonymous and yet not too far from home. During the first five years, our guests consisted mostly of out-of-towners, some coming from larger cities like Omaha. It amused us at times to speak with city dwellers whose entire world revolved around their metropolis, which had everything they could need or want.

A phone inquiry sometimes elicited the question, "Now just where is Geneva located?" It must have been reassuring to learn that it was twenty miles south of Interstate 80. Being told that they didn't need a house key when they returned from dinner was a bit unsettling for these city dwellers. A common reaction was "You mean, you don't lock your doors?"

A website on the internet was all the advertising we ever needed. In addition to the proximity of Interstate 80, Geneva's location on Highway 81, a major north/south roadway, was providential in bringing out-of-state guests to our inn. With the convenience of smart phones, it also wasn't unusual for travelers to search for lodging and reserve a room several hours before arrival.

One such guest, a young woman in her thirties, made a reservation with us from her cell phone while traveling across the country from Savannah, Georgia. Since she was craving the best fish and chips she had ever eaten, she detoured through Omaha, where she had once worked and lived. She arrived in the late evening with all her worldly possessions in her vehicle. Without a job or a place to live, she was about halfway to Idaho, her destination. We admired her adventurous spirit.

Guests arrived from more than thirty-six states and eleven foreign countries: Canada, China, France, Germany, Ireland, Norway, Pakistan, Russia, Singapore, Spain, and Taiwan. With today's technology, it has never been easier to learn about other countries and the diversity of their customs and beliefs. Yet, as we sat across the table from foreign travelers, we discovered that the similarities between us outweighed the differences.

Our most enduring cultural connection was with a young man from Spain. Due to the opening of a branch of a Barcelona-based plant in Geneva, we had the great opportunity to host him as a long-term guest. Carlos, our fourth "son," was the local plant's first manager. He lived with us for nine months. Since he left the house early in the morning and returned long after we'd gone to bed, a month had passed before he and Ken actually met. He was the perfect guest. He wanted no breakfast and left every weekend to go "birding." After he had the plant up and running, he returned to Spain. Twice annually for about ten years, he returned to check on the facility, always staying with us about eight days. Years later we spent a delightful evening with him and his family in Barcelona during our travels in 2017.

Two other plant workers from Spain also spent extended time with us. One, who was scheduled to be here for a month, brought his wife and two preschool children. The sight of their son and daughter at play with our young grandson and no common language was additional, positive proof that we're not so very different from one another.

After we had practiced our innkeeping skills on non-Nebraskans for a number of years, we began to notice that this small community's residents had awakened to the fact that there was a bed and breakfast in town which brought outsiders into the community. Local employers recommended us to people who needed long-term lodging, such as medical students and student teachers as they fulfilled requirements at the Fillmore County Hospital and the Youth Rehabilitation and Training Center.

Phone inquiries from area women's clubs, who were in search of an outing as one of their monthly activities, soon evolved into afternoon teas and tours of our home. Always a teacher, I enlightened the ladies on the history of the house and its former occupants. I also shared the story of Ken's French ancestry when I pointed out our emphasis on French breakfast entrées and French décor. They were eager to learn about the bed and breakfast experience.

Sometimes I provided each guest with a handheld fan and led a group involvement activity on the language of ladies' fans in the Victorian era. They enjoyed learning how Victorian ladies communicated their feelings and desires by different movements of a decorative fan. This activity was even more fun when done over glasses of wine in lieu of a proper English tea!

One lazy, summer afternoon, movement at the window behind the lace curtains distracted me from my reading. A wedding party was on our porch. The local photographer had become so accustomed to doing photo shoots on our property that advance warning was no longer needed. The porch and the woods were enchanting backdrops for capturing special milestones such as graduating seniors and wedding parties.

Other local groups began to use our facility. Churches sent us their ministerial candidates, three of whom accepted positions in the community. We became acquainted with these pastors before they began their ministry in Geneva. The local Rotary club reserved rooms for foreign visitors they hosted. The Odego leadership group began their annual autumn visit of local businesses with muffins and coffee at Dempster Woods.

In addition to serving these local entities, it was a blessing to participate in a small way in the important life events of guests who came to attend a family reunion, a wedding, an anniversary celebration, a grandchild's baptism or birthday party, or a relative's funeral. Through hosting the extended family of Geneva residents, we also became better acquainted with their local relatives.

It was not unusual for a Geneva resident to inquire about the possibility of bringing some of their house guests for an impromptu tour of our home. Regardless of whether we were prepared to show the house, we always complied. When a structure has been in the community longer than most other buildings and homes, it becomes the source of many connections among the people who grew up in the area. From the first days of our time in this house, we sensed that it still belonged to a lot of individuals and to the greater community. The ownership of a house of such stature came with some responsibility. We embraced every opportunity to share it with others.

To our amusement, when our guests had a connection to someone in the community, it would have been impossible to keep secret their presence at our inn. An example of this occurred one day when Charles Sloan's grandson and spouse arrived at our door. Minutes after they entered the house, the phone rang, and Senator Sloan's granddaughter wanted to speak to her cousin Bill. When I asked how she had known he was here, I learned that our next door neighbors had seen them arrive and called her to relay the news.

Another rapid means of spreading the news of guests occurred at the local coffee shop which my mother-in-law patronized. She sometimes phoned to ask if we had guests and proceeded to describe them for confirmation that she had seen them downtown. As is true in most small towns, regular patrons tend to be curious about strangers who stop at the coffee shop.

On a sadder note, one of our frequent guests with local connections became very ill during her stay with us. Other family members arrived to help the lady's husband determine a course of action. In an effort to respect their privacy and not appear intrusive at this difficult time, I went to another area of the house while they discussed the options.

A few hours later, my mother-in-law called to ask if the rescue unit had come to our house. Although I had heard no siren and was home during that time, I apparently needed someone to tell me what had transpired. This is one of the idiosyncrasies of small town living. If you aren't certain what has happened in your own life, wait a while. Someone will tell you.

Another means of becoming better acquainted with our guests' local relatives was to invite them to join us for breakfast. We'll never forget a gathering around the table with a terminally ill woman who was unable to eat much, but willing to tell fascinating family stories about raising her children. She had so many great memories to recall with her family and so little time.

In addition to welcoming overnight guests and giving private home tours, we served bridal shower brunches, hosted baby showers, graduation receptions, bridge and book clubs, Christmas parties, and anniversary dinners. Since we didn't have a commercial food license, an area restaurant catered the meals. After we had served the guests, we eagerly sat down to eat the extra portions.

Hosting these daytime events came with its own set of unpredictable elements. The day before we were to serve a large bridal shower brunch, I discovered that the toilet base in an upstairs bathroom was leaking through the ceiling into the parlor where the food would be served. There was an ironic twist: relatives of a local plumber were among the guests at the brunch. A call to our friendly carpenter, who had installed the fixtures in that bathroom, resulted in a happy outcome. He repaired the leak before guests arrived.

Bad weather provided another close call the day before a bridge club was scheduled to play cards. We were on a return trip from Boston when a winter storm halted our progress in Milwaukee. After an overnight stay there, we flew to Omaha the next morning and reached home a half hour before the card players began to arrive. Fortunately, in the event of plans gone awry, I had already prepared a frozen, ice cream cake roll before our trip. For once, my anxiety about things that never happen had paid off.

Eventually, we joined the Chamber of Commerce. We soon learned how many groups request donations or gifts from a business to support their projects. We grew to appreciate the many contributions local businesses provide for the betterment of the community. As chamber members we took our turn hosting "Business After Hours." This brought other members to our home for a social evening with refreshments. It was a unique opportunity to become better acquainted with a diverse group of people who shared the common goal of making our community an attractive, welcoming place in which to live and do business. It also enabled them to learn more about the services we offered.

In addition, we were privileged to host some very diverse special events in our home. The curiosity about Ken's vineyard generated enough local interest that the event planners of the annual July 4th community celebration asked us to host wine tastings. Since the grapes were still on the vine in our young vineyard, we twice invited an area winery to provide wine and help us to serve tastings. Many persons from surrounding communities brought visiting family members to join the locals for some "wine time." Our customary sweet treat of Raise the Flag Cookies (see the recipe section of this book) accompanied the assortment of wines.

During one of the July celebrations, the ladies of St. Joseph Catholic Church hosted a chocolate tasting/silent auction fundraiser in our home. Each chocolate lover filled a plate with an assortment of chocolate creations: truffles, chocolate dipped strawberries, chocolate covered cherries, caramel chocolate apple tartlets, cake balls. There was something to satisfy every sweet tooth and an opportunity to contribute to a worthwhile cause.

The layout of the common areas of our home lent itself to the accommodation of large groups of people, who were usually entranced by the period décor and special embellishments not found in modern homes. For that reason, hosting special events was more fun than it was work.

One year I invited my distance-learning French students to a Christmas gathering in our home. School buses from three high schools a considerable distance from Geneva transported the twenty-seven students. The activities included an informal tour of the house during a scavenger hunt with French clues, followed by Christmas caroling in French at the nursing home. It was a unique opportunity for the students and their teacher to become better acquainted while using some of their French.

My local students always welcomed an innkeeping anecdote as a diversion from class work. These too infrequent, off-topic discussions only piqued their curiosity about our lifestyle and home. The students of my senior English classes eagerly anticipated my traditional graduation gifts: pizza, a tour of our inn, and a trip to the woods. They had heard the stories and survived a term paper and a final essay exam. They arrived excited to collect their "gifts." On one occasion a young man, who was so intrigued by the bed and breakfast idea, inquired about the price of one night's lodging. When I returned from the kitchen after serving pizza and brownie sundaes, I discovered a wad of cash in the correct amount on the seat of the rocking chair. He had taken a collection from his peers to pay for an overnight stay. I assumed correctly that it was a humorous gesture, not a serious one.

Probably the most demanding and most gratifying enterprise was the preparation of our home for a tour. Every December a small number of area homes were open to the public to raise funds for the Geneva Arts' Council. The first time we agreed to participate in this event was only one year after we had moved in. Although the former owners had made some very significant, high-quality improvements, there were still many needy areas. With that in mind, we focused on the creation of an ambience which emphasized the era in which the house was built.

Some of my junior high, study hall students made snowflake-style, paper-fan ornaments and strung popcorn to decorate a large, real tree in our parlor. I placed an enormous, pottery bowl of popcorn on our smooth-top stove to hide its worn surface. An expansive length of fabric formed a drape above a bedroom mirror. It cascaded to the floor, conveniently covering a long crack in the wallpapered plaster on one wall.

Although I enjoyed the process and the event, there was probably little need to be overly concerned about staging our home. Its age and the historic significance of some of its first owners were enough to attract more than six hundred people our first year. Among them were previous owners and family members of previous owners. As they reminisced, we learned more about the improvements they had made and the surprising functions of some of the rooms: the library had been a bedroom, the pantry a bathroom, the sewing room a mother-in-law's room and a beauty shop. Descendants of "ghosts" of the past were here. They shared their stories.

Our adventure had certainly enriched our lives. A reflection I had put into my own words and cross stitched onto a sampler said it all. Pieces of vintage wallpaper, stripped from Mrs. Sloan's dressing room, bordered my message, a rustic salute to former residents and guests:

Like the shimmering droplets in the rainbow, something shines in each of our souls. We are the prism of life.

*   *   *   *   *   *

"A little piece of paradise out here in the Midlands." **Anonymous**

"This would have been the best stop along the Oregon Trail, especially the Jacuzzi. What a great surprise. Thanks for taking care and making this old house a treasure." **Kittyhawk, North Carolina**

"Muchisimas gracias por todas sus atenciones. Que les vayan con Dios!"

"Muchisimas gracias por permitirnos compartir su maravillosa casa con ustedes." **Fort Worth, Texas**

"Once again, staying with you was the highlight of my Nebraska trip. Thank you so much for your hospitality, terrific food, and making me feel like I'm part of Geneva when I'm here." **San Luis Obispo, California**

17. Love at the Inn

Bed and breakfast lodgings are often seen as romantic destinations. Guests who sought a romantic getaway arrived with love on their minds. Love for a new spouse, an old spouse, a potential spouse. If the innkeepers enjoy what they do, it should be easy for a couple to surrender responsibilities, focus on what brought them together in the first place, and deepen their relationship. We did our best to provide a setting which enabled this to take place.

For a long time Dempster Woods was the best kept secret for newly married couples in the area. They dropped off essential items and picked up a key in advance. We left the bedside lamps burning, mints on the pillows, and retreated to our basement quarters, never knowing when, or if, they had arrived until morning. We tried not to consider the possibility that the honeymooners might forget to lock the front door, making it possible for members of the wedding party to "drop in" on the bride and groom unannounced. When locked, the old Italianate was a fortress.

One weekend when we were away, a former student and her new husband heated up a breakfast entrée, which I had prepared in advance, and had the house to themselves. It was always a privilege to host a couple on their first night as man and wife and to wish them a happy life together when they departed. Sometimes an added bonus was serving brunch to families of the couple in the morning.

Surprisingly, not all newly married couples arrived in the wee hours of the morning. One warm, August afternoon, a very adventurous couple arrived on a tandem bicycle. They had been on the bike since their wedding in Nova Scotia in April, camping their way along the East Coast before heading west. She was reading *The Girl with the Dragon Tattoo* while he navigated the bike. Such trust! The next morning they mounted the bike and headed to the nearest Amtrak station where they would board, bike and all, for Oregon. When they returned to Canada, they planned to search for jobs and a place to live.

The antithesis of these youthful adventurers was the couple who came to the inn in April, 2011, to celebrate the anniversary of their trip around the world. They were a mature, married couple who had left their jobs and sold their home and all their possessions in order to spend one year circling the globe. Equipped with the essentials for a two-night stay, which included bottles of wine, four photo albums, and a journal, they embarked upon a sentimental journey. At a table on the porch, they sipped wine and shared stories for hours, prompted by the wife's reading aloud from their travel journal. At the end of two days, they had only covered half of the journal entries.

I have often thought that I was born too late. The modern world is not always a comfortable setting for an old-fashioned girl like me. If it had not come up during the booking conversation, I asked a prospective guest how many people there would be. I was not surprised, but somewhat disheartened, to discover that some couples who wished to enhance their romantic connections at our inn were not married. At times I was unaware of the nature of their relationship until they checked in. Fortunately, couples who arrived in separate vehicles was a rare occurrence.

One such pair had just met each other for the first time in the city park. They had been communicating on a dating site and had chosen Geneva for their first face-to-face encounter. After they had cleared that hurdle, they agreed to stay together at our inn. It was rather doubtful which one of the three of us was the most uncomfortable, but I sensed that it wasn't the innkeeper. We later wondered where this step of their journey had ultimately taken them.

On the other hand, the future of another young couple, who traditionally made Dempster Woods their Valentine's Day meeting place, was never in doubt. They were students whose current circumstances placed them in colleges hundreds of miles apart. They fell into a charmed routine from the first visit. Flowers always awaited her. No matter what was showing, they patronized the local movie theater, once seeing a film they had already seen. Following the movie was dinner at the Pizza Hut. They also experienced some of the other local hangouts, the coffee shop and the bar on main street. We were reasonably certain most young adults would be bored with this agenda, but this pair was intrigued.

Their first time at the theater, the young man encountered an embarrassing problem when he pulled out his credit card to pay for their tickets. This small town theater didn't take credit cards! An older lady, who overheard that they had no cash, offered to purchase tickets for them. From that moment, they were just as hooked on small-town living as they were on each other. Their last stay with us was as a married couple. What a wonderful surprise several years later when we opened a Valentine card with a photo of them with their new son. They now have three sons. A very happy bookmark in their life story!

Guests who came to celebrate an anniversary sometimes requested an appointment for a massage. An enterprising, local masseuse willingly toted her heavy, portable table upstairs for an on-site treatment in the guests' room. A candlelit breakfast awaited the couple in the morning.

On one occasion when two couples had reserved rooms, I neglected to check my notes before I greeted them the next morning. Eager to surprise them, I lit the candles on the table.

"Happy Anniversary!" I exclaimed exuberantly when the first couple descended the stairs.

The wife was quick to set me straight, "It's not our anniversary."

Oops! Wrong couple!

A surprise 50th anniversary dinner party was the most memorable, intimate gathering we ever hosted. The honored couple had owned our home for nineteen years and raised their four children in it. Three generations of family were present to celebrate the memories of a very special time in their lives. It was poignantly obvious that this dwelling had been a place where love and laughter resided. As we served them a catered dinner and listened to their stories, for this one evening, we too became part of their story.

*   *   *   *   *   *

"We had a wonderful Valentine's weekend here! This room is gorgeous and I love the stained glass! I can't wait to come visit again." **Kearney, Nebraska**

"Another wonderful Valentine's weekend at Dempster Woods and our 8 month wedding anniversary! Thanks so much." **Omaha, Nebraska**

"Thank you for opening your home to Tim and me on our 5 year wedding anniversary. We loved lounging on the porch and in our room. The quiet and homey atmosphere gave us a chance, as my husband so accurately stated, to notice each other again." **Anonymous**

"We spent our wedding night in the Rainbow Room. Your whole place is beautiful! What a great memory of our first married night!" **Narka, Kansas**

18. Host or Guest

Many years ago Ken and I watched *Babettie's Feast,* an Oscar-winning Danish film based on Karen Blixen's book. Babette, a refugee from revolutionary Paris, offers to prepare a festive French dinner in honor of her hosts' deceased father. His daughters have known nothing but a very religious, unremarkable, meager lifestyle in a small, fishing village. Babette's plans dispel the gloominess and drudgery of their dreary existence as she prepares a memorial meal of sensually exotic entrées. Although the film made an impact on us, we never imagined that, like Babette, future guests in our home would light up our lives and energize our spirits.

In the early years of innkeeping, this moving drama resurfaced as a teaching point for an inspirational message on the front of our church's Sunday bulletin. I laminated multiple copies and displayed them in each of our guest rooms.

The effect of Babette's story didn't end there. At the top of the stairs hung one of the pedestals from a Station of the Cross. It was a souvenir from our old church building. Angelic cherubs covered this elaborate base on which a statue grouping had once rested. As I pondered what to place above this pedestal, I recalled a scriptural passage which had always held special meaning for me. Before our first tour of homes, I had painstakingly cross stitched this passage in gold, metallic thread. The completed project hung on the wall above the pedestal. It proved prophetic for us.

> Do not neglect hospitality, for through it
> some have unknowingly entertained angels.
> (Hebrews 13: 2, *New American Bible*)

In the early stages of innkeeping, I considered this sampler to be merely an appropriate decorative touch which guests would see as they ascended the stairs. Our business brochures read "We invite you to fall in love with life again. We want our guests to share a little of themselves and to leave refreshed and enchanted with life as it was a century ago."

We made every effort to become hosts who offered an optimal escape in every regard: comfort, sustenance, peace, inspiration for living. However, it soon became obvious that guests gave us much more than the weekend package we offered them.

After guests departed the physical preparation for the next round of guests was always our first priority. Days or weeks after we had cleared away the breakfast clutter, loaded the dishwasher, emptied the trash, and gathered the laundry, we were ready to reflect on the guests and our time with them. What did they share of themselves? What did they leave behind? It was much more than mountains of dirty linens and a sink full of dirty dishes.

Reflection on this idea eventually altered our perception of innkeeping. As more guests passed in and out of our front door, some surprised us with tokens of their appreciation: a miniature, electric china teapot, an antique, wicker mail holder, jasmine tea and a scarf from Taiwan, cookies from Barcelona, a Williams-Sonoma *After Dinner Cookbook*, two jars of homemade salsa. Other gifts arrived later via parcel post: a Trader Joe's care package from California (because we had whined about not having one in Nebraska at that time), an artist's rendition of Monet's Garden on a thank you card (from our first guest), wine and jam from Whidbey Island, Washington (an acknowledgment of the wine Ken made from his personal vineyard), a *Debussy at Dawn* CD to supplement our breakfast mood music, and quilting fabric from a guest's deceased mother's stash.

While we delighted in the irony of receiving spontaneous gifts from guests who had paid us for lodging, we cherished more the intangible things, like conversation. Most liked to talk about themselves and their families. One question led to a thousand words. After we had exchanged the basics (number of children, careers), we turned to common challenges: aging parents, children's journeys to adulthood, being older grandparents. Guests and hosts alike discovered that it was incredibly easy to tell strangers things one wouldn't always share with friends and family. It was very encouraging and therapeutic to learn that we all traveled the same road with surprisingly similar detours.

In addition to learning that we all have common life concerns, we shared memorable travel experiences and favorite restaurants with one another. The conversation became quite lively when we learned that our guests had also been to France. Our accounts of travel on our own in France were the fuel for much laughter as we reminisced about many a "faux pas." Consequently, we all then poked fun at ourselves and at the Frenchmen's reactions to our cultural missteps.

Even rarer than serving a table of Francophiles was hosting track and field fanatics. The discovery of such an elite minority in football country didn't happen often enough, but track talk accelerated our heartbeats and preempted conversation on all other topics. Since Ken had been a track and cross country coach and a track high jump official, he always contributed to this engaging exchange.

Another pleasant perk guests provided was free professional advice: a botanist's ability to identify a shrub Ken had transplanted from his great-grandparents' farmyard; reassurance from an architect that the crack along the bricks in the house façade was not a potential problem; a dental hygienist's simple solution to my intermittent locking jaw. She had solved her own similar problem by flying to the west coast to receive help to alleviate this ailment. I followed her advice and began to chew on both sides of my mouth simultaneously. Soon my agony ended. I should have offered her a free night's lodging!

Guests soon discovered that a sure way to get my attention was to reveal their love for books. One couple, who stayed multiple times, spent time reading in the library or on the porch during the evenings. As an avid reader, I was interested in the current choices of the local book clubs who met at our home. Even though I hadn't read their selection, the group always invited me to join them during their discussion. At the breakfast table, family groups sometimes engaged in lively discussions of books they had recently read. Guests who perused the selections in our bookcase expressed their approval.

Previous guests had written four of those books. A heroic, teenage girl wrote an inspirational book about the challenges of living with the aftereffects of lyme disease. Another nonfiction book was a tribute to the author's heritage and an account of her parents' journey, part of which took place in Geneva. One guest had written a mystery thriller.

The transformation of my sewing room into an extra guest room for one writer resulted in another avenue of free advertising and some personalized reading material for other guests: an issue of *Nebraska Life Magazine* on the coffee table contained her article and a photo of our inn.

Music is another pastime Ken and I both enjoy. While he prefers to listen to it, I prefer making it. He taught himself to play the harmonica, an instrument he can easily take with him for those long hours in a farm vehicle. I have played the piano all my life and have made an effort to learn the guitar. Perhaps the piano and the guitar in our common rooms prompted guests to spontaneously perform a number of times, in varying degrees of expertise.

One of those times occurred when four retired women, who had been college friends, reunited at Dempster Woods. To their delight, Javier, a handsome Spaniard, whose local work made him a long-term guest, strummed guitar chords for their sing-along requests. Another guest, who traveled with his guitar, offered an unsolicited serenade following breakfast one morning. And, of course, we will never forget the mostly male, memorable family of ten who held their own jam session, piano and guitars, at the midnight hour.

Undoubtedly, the most astonishing musical performance by guests in our home was the Baptist college choir who offered a private concert in our parlor. They stood on the open stairway above the piano and filled the room with inspirational music, something they had been doing in churches across the country all summer.

That evening one of the young singers returned to the house after a run. Dripping with perspiration, he sat at the dining room table with me. Bibles in hand, we shared the Baptist and the Catholic versions of the "faith versus works" topic. Each of us gained a better understanding of the rationale behind our diverse beliefs. Weeks later Ken and I would recall the selflessness and youthful zeal of these young adults when we listened to the two CDs they had given us.

Perhaps the most priceless of all our guests' gifts was the gift of hope. As people crossed our paths, we became better acquainted with the frailty of the human body and the indestructibility of the human spirit. This rang true with me one morning when I greeted an anniversary couple at breakfast for the first time. I had not checked them in the previous evening.

Although I tried not to stare at the young man's face, which resembled a raised relief road map, I made the unnerving discovery that he had no ears. How does one act normal when confronted unexpectedly with a burn victim? We were humbled to serve them and hear their story. They had come to celebrate a fifth anniversary. What courage it must take for them to face a world which overvalues physical beauty. What a privilege for us to witness a profound example of the proverbs "Love is blind" and "Beauty is only skin deep."

Obviously, we never knew what to expect when people gathered at our table, but we knew it would be special in some way. In today's culture, gathering at the table for a meal served in courses is a rare occurrence in most people's lives. In her book *Simple Social Graces,* Linda S. Lichter says that in Victorian times daily meals were special affairs treated like special occasions. We hoped breakfasts at Dempster Woods felt like special occasions.

Whenever the talk at the table grew quiet immediately after we had served the first entrée and retreated to the kitchen, I listened for the beginning of a meal blessing. It gave me hope that in this "grab and go" era some still practiced the ritual of thankfulness for food with a prayer.

It was spiritually uplifting to serve people who shared values similar to ours. An outstanding example of this was a Jehovah's Witness group who stayed with us for an entire week. The woman who had phoned from Idaho for reservations for eight persons was initially rather evasive when I asked if they were here to visit relatives. Before she finally revealed the purpose of their visit, she said, "We're reputable people." I believed her.

Following breakfast each morning, they prepared for their daily mission of calling on area residents by gathering in a circle on our porch, books in hand, in thoughtful study and meditation. Before they departed on their final morning, the leader told me he had to get cash for payment and would return with it later that day. It was a significant amount, and his promise required of me just as much trust. At five in the afternoon he was at the door, cash in hand. I silently chastised myself for my skepticism and lack of faith in humanity. I thanked God for their impressive example of commitment and perseverance.

Perseverance was Jim's middle name. Jim was a regular visitor at Dempster Woods. On his last stay with us, Ken told him that he could take home a volunteer pine tree growing in one of the flower beds. On a warm, humid summer day, Jim, sweat streaming down his face, insisted on digging up the baby tree himself, even though Ken had offered to do it for him. Oxygen tank in tow, Jim managed to uproot the tenacious, little pine. He and his family had traveled in Europe and toted the large tank wherever they went. His perseverance took my breath away!

Another guest listened to my saga of current health issues and sensed my life view as seeing the glass as half-empty. When I walked her to her car, she retrieved a prayer pebble from her pocket and placed it in the palm of my hand. Sally had terminal cancer. The imperfections of my current state of health paled by comparison. She had shared more than her story. She had given me a sense of hope and an adjusted perspective. Ultimately, I passed the pebble on to someone else who needed it. St. Frances de Sales wrote, "Since God often sends us inspirations by means of angels, we should frequently return our aspirations to God by means of the same messengers."

Examples of hope in the faces of today's young adults have probably inspired us more than anything else. Two consecutive years in January we hosted a houseful of university resident assistants and their supervisor. These were occasions of a yearly retreat, a time to assess and improve procedures for handling the academic and social lives of the students in their charge. We abandoned some stereotypical misconceptions about today's young adults the moment they began to brainstorm and share plans for helping their peers. In comparison to the college students of our day, they were from a star-studded galaxy. Unflinchingly, they faced continually shifting circumstances. Their politeness, intelligence, and refreshing individuality were remarkable.

After fourteen years of service to guests in our home, we closed the inn. As we look back on that time, we know it changed our lives. It was not a living. It was a way of life. By opening our doors to strangers, two rather private people experienced many fascinating and stimulating interactions with an ever-changing set of "angels" who played hosts to us. These "angels" revealed to us that throughout this life, like the characters in *Babette's Feast*, we are all hosts and guests, with the common goal of helping one another to the next destination.

*   *   *   *   *   *

"The conversation is always a high point of our visit." **Lincoln, Nebraska**

"Thank you very much for another wonderful visit here. Being able to listen to Vivaldi's 'Four Seasons' during breakfast was especially nice this time." **Lilburn, Georgia**

"Thank you. You are angels!" **Windom, Minnesota**

"Just like a good bed and breakfast or a good road trip for that matter--this overnight forged connections with the other guests, weaving a common thread through time and place. Over morning coffee, in what ended up like a tic-tac-toe match, I discovered I went to college in the same Texas town one of the other guests was from. Another guest lived in a Colorado city where yet another boarder owned a house. I wasn't even the only writer in the bunch. Not only was there a copy of the most recent *Nebraska Life Magazine* on the parlor table, but a copy of another guest's first novel, a murder mystery. Obviously, Sandy and Ken know a little something about bringing people together in Nebraska: put them in a room together with hot coffee and the rest will work itself out." **Lisa Munger,** *Nebraska Life Magazine*

Epilogue

In 2007 Sandra concluded her teaching career. Our lives took on a new dimension in 2008 with the arrival of our first grandchild. Four months later a granddaughter was born. In another fifteen months, a third grandchild joined our extended family. After believing for many years that we would never have grandchildren, we were eager to begin this era of our life together. While we still enjoyed entertaining guests, we soon discovered that keeping grandchildren overnight with paying guests in the house was going to be a tricky task, especially in the morning. We certainly didn't want to turn away any opportunities to have our grandchildren. The new direction of our lives was obvious. In June 2012 we hosted Ken's 50-year high school class reunion and our last guests.

Life in such a large home with its unoccupied spaces and no more shared stories soon lost its charm for Sandra. She was ready for a more convenient, smaller space. Ken was a little more reluctant to change residences because he was already living in his "dream home." A happy wife means a happy husband! In 2015, after an incredible adventure of 19 years, he agreed to put the old Italianate on the market.

At the end of the year, we moved into a ranch-style house just three blocks down the street. At that time our "new" dwelling was 30 years old, almost 100 years younger than the old one. In April of 2016, the new owners moved into our former home. It is being lovingly maintained as a private residence as they continue to restore and improve the house and the outdoor property.

The adjustment to a vastly different dwelling was seamless for Sandra who loved the attached garage and main floor bedroom. In time Ken agreed that the move was a timely one and a good choice. He now has his own man cave, almost the entire lower level.

He sometimes passes the old house on his daily morning walk. The older grandchildren miss the "old" house with its front and back stairs and the endless places to hide from one another. After all, it was where they first became acquainted with their grandparents. We hope they also recall our treks into the woods to explore and pick up pine cones. Sandra remembers gathering them for decorations for our son's wedding rehearsal dinner.

Although we have no regrets, as the years pass, the memories become more poignant. It was, and hopefully still is, a peaceful place that feeds the soul. A place where love abides. Every holiday season Sandra still envisions the seven Christmas trees, one in each front window of the old house, a welcoming sight in a space to be shared. We are so grateful for the opportunity God planned for us.

RECIPES YOU WILL LOVE TO SHARE

"There is no love sincerer than the love of food."
George Bernard Shaw

Breakfast Entrées

French Crêpes
(our signature dish)

1 cup flour
1/8 teaspoon salt
1 tablespoon sugar
1 cup milk
2 tablespoons melted butter
2 eggs

Sift together flour, salt, sugar. Beat eggs and stir in milk and butter. Place all ingredients in a blender and blend until smooth, using a spatula to stir away any flour clinging to the sides. Chill mixture for one hour in the refrigerator. If the batter is not the consistency of heavy cream, add more milk and blend again.

NOTE: If the first crêpe is too thick, you may want to adjust the amount poured into the pan and/or add more milk to thin the batter. This makes about 18 crêpes.

Oil an 8 or 9-inch non-stick skillet or a seasoned cast iron skillet and heat on medium heat until very hot. (A cast iron skillet should only be used for crêpes. After using it, wipe it out with a paper towel. Do not wash it.)

1. Heat the skillet on moderate heat until it is very hot.
2. Remove excess oil from the skillet.
3. Pour about one quarter cup of batter into the pan center; quickly remove the skillet from the burner and rotate it to coat the pan with the batter.

4. Place the skillet back on the burner, cooking the crêpe about one minute or until it is dry and the bottom is lightly browned.
5. Using a spatula, turn the crêpe and cook on the second side about 30 seconds. The first side will be the outside of the crêpe because it browns nicely.
6. Stack the crêpes on a clean towel and wrap them up for reheating when ready to serve them. You may also freeze them in appropriate units separated by wax paper.

Crêpe Fillings

Lemon Ricotta Filling
8 ounces ricotta cheese
lemon zest from 1 lemon
¼ cup powdered sugar
1 teaspoon vanilla
2-4 teaspoons heavy cream

Whip all of the ingredients in a mixer until creamy. Spoon 2 tablespoons into one of the corners of a crêpe and fold the crêpe into fourths. Garnish with mixed berries and powered sugar sprinkled on top.

Banana Rum Crêpe Sauce
1 cup brown sugar
2 tablespoons dark corn syrup
2 tablespoons rum
2 tablespoons butter
½ cup heavy cream
1 teaspoon vanilla extract

Bring to a boil the above ingredients. Reduce heat and simmer 2 minutes. Set aside to cool.

Toppings and fillings
bananas
chopped pecans
sugar and cinnamon
powdered sugar

Slice bananas and place slices down the center of each crêpe. Drizzle with a little of the cooled sauce. Sprinkle with cinnamon and sugar to taste. Roll up each crêpe and place on a serving plate. Sprinkle with slices of bananas and chopped pecans. Drizzle with more rum sauce and sprinkle with powdered sugar.

Spinach Filling and Ham Sauce

Spinach Filling
1 cup chopped onion
2 tablespoons butter
1 package (10 oz.) frozen,
    chopped spinach, thawed
1 cup grated Swiss cheese
1 tablespoon Dijon mustard
¼ teaspoon salt
¼ teaspoon ground nutmeg

Saute onion in butter until tender, not brown. Add spinach and cook until it is tender and there is no moisture. Stir in the remaining ingredients.

Ham Sauce
2 tablespoons butter
2 tablespoons flour
¼ teaspoon salt
1 cup milk
½ cup half and half
2 tablespoons Dijon mustard
1 ½ cups diced fully cooked ham

Melt butter in a saucepan. Stir in flour and salt. Add remaining ingredients except for ham. Cook while stirring constantly until thickened. Add ham and heat.

Fill each crêpe with about ¼ cup of the Spinach Filling and roll up. Spoon Ham Sauce over the crêpes.

Quiche Lorraine

1 pie crust (9-inch)
1 tablespoon bacon drippings
1 cup thinly sliced onions
1 ½ cups cubed Gruyere or Swiss Cheese
4 slices crisp bacon, crumbled
4 large eggs
2 cups heavy cream or 1 cup each milk and cream
¼ teaspoon ground pepper
¼ teaspoon ground nutmeg
¼ teaspoon salt

Line a pie pan with the pie crust and bake 5 minutes. Cook the onions in the bacon drippings until they are transparent. Cover the pastry with the cheese, onions, and bacon. Combine the remaining ingredients and pour over the top. Bake in a preheated 450 degree oven for 10 minutes. Reduce heat to 350 degrees and bake until a knife inserted into the center comes out clean (about 25 minutes).

Overnight Apple French Toast Casserole

1 loaf (10oz.) French bread, cut into cubes
8 eggs
3 cups milk
4 teaspoons sugar
1 teaspoon vanilla

3/4 teaspoon salt
¼ teaspoon cinnamon
1 or 2 finely chopped Granny Smith apples

Topping
2 tablespoons butter, cubed
3 tablespoons sugar
2 teaspoons ground cinnamon
½ cup chopped pecans (to be added after baking)

Place bread cubes in a greased 13x9x2-inch baking dish. Beat eggs, milk, sugar, vanilla, salt, and cinnamon until frothy. Add chopped apples. Pour mixture over the bread. Cover and refrigerate overnight.

Remove from refrigerator 30 minutes before baking. Dot with butter. Combine sugar and cinnamon; sprinkle over the top. Cover and bake at 350 degrees for 45-50 minutes or until a knife inserted in the center comes out clean. Sprinkle chopped pecans over the top. Let stand for 5 minutes. Serve with maple syrup.

Lydia's Strawberry Custard Muffins

4 English muffins
4 ounces cream cheese
4 tablespoons strawberry preserves
2 cups milk
½ cup sugar
2 teaspoons vanilla
6 eggs
2 tablespoons butter
cinnamon
1 quart fresh strawberries, sprinkled with sugar

Allow cream cheese to soften. Divide muffins and spread bottom half of each with cream cheese. Top with preserves. Replace top. Place in greased 9-inch square baking dish.

Combine the milk, sugar, vanilla, and eggs and beat until frothy. Pour over the muffins. Refrigerate at least 4 hours or overnight.

Preheat oven to 325 degrees. Spoon egg mixture over muffins. Then top each with a pat of butter and sprinkle all with cinnamon. Bake 45 minutes or until set.

Slice the strawberries, leaving a few whole with leaves for garnish. Sprinkle with sugar and allow to set until custard is finished baking. Garnish each muffin with strawberries.

Lydia Johnson Inn, Hermann, Missouri

Blueberry Filled French Toast

6 slices Texas Toast, crust removed and cubed
1 (8 ounce) package cream cheese, cubed
½ cup fresh blueberries
6 eggs
3 tablespoons pure maple syrup
1 cup milk

Preheat oven to 350 degrees. Coat an 8 or 9-inch baking dish with non-stick vegetable spray. Place half of the bread cubes in bottom of baking dish. Evenly place cream cheese cubes over top of bread. Scatter blueberries over cream cheese. Place the remaining bread over blueberries. In a large bowl, beat together eggs, syrup and milk. Pour egg mixture over bread in baking dish. Cover and chill overnight. Remove from refrigerator. Remove cover. Cover with aluminum foil. Bake at 350 degrees for 30 minutes. Remove foil and bake for 30 additional minutes. Remove from oven and let set for 10 minutes. Cut French toast into serving pieces. Pour warm blueberry sauce over each piece.

Blueberry Sauce

½ cup water
½ cup sugar
1 tablespoon cornstarch
1 cup blueberries
2 teaspoons butter, melted
¼ teaspoon orange extract or zest

In small saucepan, combine water, sugar, cornstarch, and ½ cup of blueberries. Cook over medium heat until mixture thickens, stirring frequently. Add the remaining blueberries and butter. Add orange extract or zest. Mix to blend.

Hancock House Bed and Breakfast, Dubuque, Iowa

Breakfast Pizza

1 pound sausage, browned and drained
1 (8 ounce) package refrigerated crescent rolls
2 cups loose pack frozen shredded potatoes (thawed)
1 cup grated mozzarella or cheddar cheese
5 eggs
¼ cup milk
1/8 teaspoon salt
1/8 teaspoon pepper
2 tablespoons Parmesan cheese

Separate crescent rolls into 8 triangles. Arrange on 12-inch ungreased pizza pan with points toward center. Press dough together to seal perforations and press dough onto sides of pan to form a crust. Spoon sausage over crust. Sprinkle potatoes, then cheese, on top. In a small bowl mix eggs, milk, salt, and pepper. Pour over all. Sprinkle top with Parmesan cheese. Bake at 350 degrees 25-30 minutes.

Broccoli Oven Omelet (Eggs Italiano)

9 eggs
10 ounces frozen broccoli, chopped*
1/3 cup finely chopped onion
¼ cup grated Parmesan cheese
2 tablespoons milk
½ teaspoon salt
½ teaspoon dried basil
¼ teaspoon garlic powder
1 medium tomato, cut into 6 slices
¼ cup grated Parmesan cheese

*NOTE: chopped uncooked spinach may be substituted for the broccoli.

Beat eggs with whisk in bowl until light and fluffy. Stir in broccoli, onion, ¼ cup Parmesan cheese, milk, salt, basil, and garlic powder. Top with tomato slices and sprinkle with ¼ cup Parmesan cheese.

Pour into ungreased 11x7x2-inch glass baking pan. Bake uncovered in 325 degree oven until set, 25-30 minutes.

Frosted Fruit Salad (6 servings)

2 large apples, cut into ¾ inch cubes
2 medium firm bananas, sliced
2 teaspoons lemon juice
1 carton (6 ounces) fat-free reduced sugar raspberry yogurt
¼ cup raisins or dried cranberries
1 tablespoon sunflower seeds
In a large bowl, combine apples and bananas. Sprinkle with lemon juice; toss to coat. Stir in the yogurt, raisins, and sunflower seeds.

Taste of Home, **courtesy of Ann Fox**

Bread, Rolls, and Coffeecakes

Sour Cream Banana Muffins

½ cup butter
1 cup sugar
2 eggs
1 teaspoon vanilla extract
1½ cups all-purpose flour
1 teaspoon baking soda
½ teaspoon salt
1 cup mashed bananas
½ cup chopped walnuts
½ cup sour cream

Cream butter with the sugar. Add eggs and vanilla. Add dry ingredients; mix. Add the mashed bananas, nuts, and sour cream. Bake in a greased loaf pan in a 350 degree oven for 1 hour; 12 regular muffins, bake for 20 minutes; 6 jumbo muffins, bake for 25-30 minutes.

Bed and Breakfasts and More

French Breakfast Puffs

1/3 cup soft shortening
½ cup sugar
1 egg
1½ cups flour
½ teaspoon salt
1½ teaspoons baking powder
¼ teaspoon nutmeg
½ cup milk

Topping
6 tablespoons melted butter

½ cup or more of sugar
1 teaspoon cinnamon

Mix shortening, sugar and egg. Sift dry ingredients and stir into creamed mixture alternately with milk. Fill greased muffin tins 2/3 full. Bake 20-25 minutes at 350 degrees. After baked, roll in butter, cinnamon, and sugar mixture.

Carrot Zucchini Bread/Muffins

2½ cups sugar
6 large eggs
2½ cups vegetable oil
1½ teaspoons vanilla
4 cups all-purpose flour
4 teaspoons baking powder
1 teaspoon salt
1½ teaspoons cinnamon
1½ teaspoons ground cloves
½ teaspoon ground nutmeg
2 cups grated raw carrots
2 cups grated raw zucchini
2 cups chopped walnuts
1 teaspoon grated orange rind

Preheat oven to 350 degrees. Lightly grease three 8½x4x2-inch loaf pans, two 9x5x3-inch loaf pans, or jumbo muffin tins.

In a large bowl beat sugar, eggs, oil, and vanilla. In a separate bowl sift together flour, baking powder, salt, and spices. Stir this mixture into the wet mixture until just blended. Fold in carrots, zucchini, nuts, and orange rind all at once. Pour batter into prepared pans and place them in the oven. Bake 50-60 minutes for larger loaves or until toothpick inserted into the center comes out clean. Bake jumbo muffins for about 25-30 minutes. Remove pans from oven to wire racks and cool 15 minutes. Then remove from pans. Place loaves on their sides until completely cooled.

Camilla Lauber

French Almond Croissants

1 cup ground almonds*
½ cup powdered sugar
1 egg white
½ teaspoon almond extract
2 (8 ounce) cans crescent dinner rolls
2 tablespoons butter, softened

1 egg white, slightly beaten
1 teaspoon water
¼ cup sliced almonds

Glaze
½ cup powdered sugar
½ teaspoon almond extract
1 tablespoon butter, softened
2-3 teaspoons milk

Heat oven to 375 degrees. Lightly grease 2 cookie sheets. In small bowl, combine ground almonds, powdered sugar, egg white, and almond extract. Separate dough into 16 triangles. Spread scant ½ teaspoon butter over each triangle to within ½ inch of edges. Spread about 2 teaspoons almond mixture over butter. Roll up, starting at shorter side of triangle and rolling to the opposite point. Place rolls point side down on cookie sheets; curve each into a crescent shape. Combine remaining egg white and water; brush over rolls. Place sliced almonds on rolls. Bake at 375 degrees for 10-15 minutes or until golden brown. In a small bowl, blend glaze ingredients until smooth; drizzle over warm rolls.

*NOTE: a little less than a whole cup of almonds will equal 1 cup ground almonds.

Raspberry Almond Coffee Cake

Combine and set aside:
1 cup fresh raspberries
3 tablespoons brown sugar

Combine dry ingredients:

1 cup flour
1/3 cup sugar
½ teaspoon baking powder
¼ teaspoon baking soda
1/8 teaspoon salt

Combine wet ingredients:

½ cup sour cream
2 tablespoons melted butter
1 teaspoon vanilla extract
1 egg

Add wet ingredients to dry until moistened. Spray an 8-inch spring form pan with vegetable spray; layer 2/3 of the batter, raspberry mixture, and the remaining 1/3 of the batter. Top with ¼ cup sliced almonds. Bake at 350 degrees for 40 minutes until a toothpick in the center comes out clean. Cool. Remove from pan.

Glaze
¼ cup powdered sugar
1 teaspoon milk
¼ teaspoon vanilla
¼ cup sliced almonds

Mix sugar, milk, vanilla. Drizzle over coffeecake. Sprinkle with almonds.

Danish Almond Puff

½ cup butter
1 cup flour
½ teaspoon salt
2 tablespoons cold water

Mix flour and salt. Use pastry blender to add butter. Add water. Spread on a large pizza pan.

Filling
½ cup butter
1 cup water
½ teaspoon salt
1 cup flour
3 eggs, room temperature
½ teaspoon almond extract

Bring butter, salt, and water to a boil. Remove from heat. Quickly beat flour into mixture with a mixer for 30-60 seconds. Add eggs one at a time, beating after each. Beat until batter no longer looks slimy. Add extract. Spread over the crust. Bake at 450 degrees for 30 minutes.

Glaze
2 tablespoons butter, softened
1½ cups powdered sugar
1-2 tablespoons water
1½ teaspoons vanilla extract
½ cup sliced almonds

Mix the first four ingredients and glaze coffee cake while it is still warm. Sprinkle with almonds. Serve immediately.

Sunflower and Spice Granola Bars

1½ cups rolled oats
¾ cup roasted sunflower seeds
½ cup coconut
¼ cup toasted wheat germ
¼ cup whole-wheat flour
¼ teaspoon ground cinnamon
1/8 teaspoon ground nutmeg
½ cup margarine or butter
½ cup packed brown sugar
1/3 cup honey

In a bowl, stir together oats, sunflower seeds, coconut, wheat germ, flour, cinnamon, and nutmeg. Set aside.

In a saucepan over low heat, or in a bowl in a microwave oven, melt margarine. Stir in brown sugar and honey; bring to boiling. Remove from heat. Pour margarine mixture over oats mixture. Stir until well coated. Press into greased, 8-inch square baking pan. Sprinkle with additional sunflower seeds and coconut, if desired.

Bake at 350 degrees for 35-45 minutes, until slightly browned around the edges. Remove from oven. While still warm, press surface gently with back of a spoon to flatten and score into bars with a knife. Cool completely before cutting into bars. Makes 12 bars.

Easter Bunny Rolls

2 packages active dry yeast
¼ cup warm water (110-115 degrees)
1 cup 2 % milk
½ cup shortening
2 eggs
1/3 cup sugar

¼ cup orange juice
2 tablespoons grated orange peel
1 teaspoon salt
5-5½ cups all-purpose flour

Dissolve yeast in water. Add milk, shortening, eggs, sugar, orange juice and peel, salt, and 3 cups of the flour. Beat until smooth. Add enough remaining flour to make a soft dough. Knead on floured surface until smooth and elastic (6-8 minutes). Place in a greased bowl, turning once to grease the top. Cover and let rise in a warm place until doubled (1 hour). Punch down and roll into a rectangle ½ inch thick. Use a pizza cutter to cut strips to form bunnies: roll 5 inch strips into a spiral for the head and 10 inch strips for the body. Pinch off a small ball of dough for the tail and 2 short strips for the ears. Place 2 inches apart on greased baking sheets. Cover and let rise until doubled (30 minutes). Bake at 375 degrees 12-15 minutes.

Glaze
2 cups powdered sugar
¼ cup water
1 tablespoon orange marmalade
½ teaspoon butter, softened

Mix together until smooth and drizzle over cooled bunnies.

Appetizers

Avocado Yogurt Dip

¾ cup plain yogurt
½ cup chopped red onion
3 tablespoons fresh cilantro, chopped
1 tablespoon jalapeno, chopped (opt.)
2 tablespoons lime juice
1 tablespoon ground cumin
½ teaspoon salt
3 avocados, peeled, chopped, and mashed
1 clove garlic, minced

Mix all the ingredients and refrigerate for 8 hours before serving.

Olive Nut Spread

6 ounces cream cheese, softened
½ cup mayonnaise
1 cup chopped green salad olives
½ cup chopped pecans
2 tablespoons olive juice
dash of pepper

Mix cream cheese and mayonnaise. Chop olives until you have one cupful. Add to the creamed mixture with olive juice and pepper. Stir well. Put mixture in a pint fruit jar with a lid and refrigerate for at least 24 hours. The mixture will thicken. Spread on unflavored crackers of your choice.

Beer Sauced Links

2 pounds fully cooked Polish sausage, cut into ½
    inch pieces.
1 cup beer

¼ cup brown sugar
2 tablespoons cornstarch
¼ cup cider vinegar
¼ cup prepared mustard
1 tablespoon prepared horseradish

In a skillet combine sausage and beer. Cover and simmer 10 minutes. Combine brown sugar and cornstarch. Stir in vinegar, mustard, and horseradish. Add to sausages and cook until bubbly. Turn into a crock pot on low. Serve warm with toothpicks.

Darline Rathje

Tote'm Rolls

1 pound ground beef
1 (1 ounce) envelope dry onion soup
¾ teaspoon crushed oregano
1/8 teaspoon garlic salt
½ cup ketchup
2 cans of refrigerated crescent rolls
1 cup shredded Mozzarella cheese
poppy seeds

Brown ground beef and drain. Stir in onion soup, oregano, garlic salt, and ketchup. Cool mixture. Meanwhile, separate the crescent rolls into 8 rectangles. Seal perforations. Spoon cooled hamburger mixture onto lengthwise side of each rectangle. Sprinkle with cheese. Roll up from one long edge to the other, jelly roll fashion. Bring ends together to form a donut shape. Seal ends tightly. Sprinkle with poppy seeds. Place "donuts" on an ungreased baking sheet and bake at 375 degrees for 15 minutes or until golden. Serve hot or cold.

Omaha World-Herald

Hot Ham Sandwiches

Assemble the following into sandwiches:
1 pound shaved ham
24 slices Swiss cheese
24 small buns or Hawaiian Rolls

Mix the following ingredients and bring to a boil:

2 sticks oleo
4 tablespoons Worcestershire Sauce
4 tablespoons dry mustard
8 tablespoons brown sugar
2 tablespoons poppy seeds

Pour over sandwiches and marinate 4 hours or more. Then bake covered at 350 degrees for 25 minutes. Uncover and bake 5 more minutes.

Tomato Salsa

12 cups cut tomatoes, peeled and quartered
4 large onions, ground and drained
5 green peppers, ground and drained
8 cloves garlic, minced
8 fresh jalapenos, ground and drained
5 tablespoons dark vinegar
1 tablespoon cayenne pepper
1 tablespoon chili powder
1 teaspoon paprika
¼ cup corn syrup
5 tablespoons sugar

Simmer the above for two hours. Cook until thick. Place in jars. Boil in a hot water bath for 20 minutes.

Diane Fisher

Beef Jerky

1½ pounds lean brisket, sliced for jerky
1 teaspoon seasoned salt
1/3 teaspoon garlic powder
1/3 teaspoon black pepper
1 teaspoon MSG
1 teaspoon onion powder
1 teaspoon liquid smoke
1/3 cup Worcestershire Sauce
1/3 cup soy sauce
½ cup water

Layer brisket in a glass container. Mix the remaining ingredients and pour over the brisket. Refrigerate for several days. Drain and place brisket strips on a rack in the oven at 150 degrees. Bake and baste for 8 hours.

Lee Kamler, mother

Spicy TV Mix

4 cups Cheerios
4 cups Kix
6 cups Rice Chex
6 cups Wheat Chex
5 ounces slim pretzels
2 (8.75 ounce) cans mixed nuts
2 tablespoons Worcestershire Sauce
1 teaspoon garlic salt
1 teaspoon celery salt
1 teaspoon chili powder
1 teaspoon paprika
1 (8 ounce) container Parmesan cheese
1 pound butter

Melt butter in a saucepan. Add seasoning and cheese. Bring to a boil. Pour over the cereals, pretzels, and nuts. Stir. Place in a 200 degree oven for 2 hours, stirring every half hour. Store in Ziplock bags.

Aunt Bernie DiNatale

Main Dishes

Italian Spaghetti Sauce

1½ pounds ground beef
1 large onion, chopped
1 green pepper, chopped (opt.)
2 small cans tomato paste
1 small can tomato sauce
2 cloves garlic, minced
1 cup water
½ cup cooking sherry or red wine
2 tablespoons sugar
1 teaspoon salt
1 teaspoon oregano
1 bay leaf

Brown beef, onion, and pepper. Drain meat and set aside. Put remaining ingredients in pan and cook slowly until mixture begins to thicken. Return meat to pan. Cook slowly over low heat for 1 hour.

Skillet Macaroni and Beef Sauté

1/4 cup cooking oil
1 pound lean ground beef
2 cups elbow macaroni
1 clove garlic, minced
½ cup chopped green pepper
¼ cup chopped onion

Brown meat in oil; then add macaroni, stirring and cooking until slightly yellow. Add onion, garlic, green pepper, and sauté until onion is transparent. Drain off grease.

Add the following ingredients to the above mixture:

1½ teaspoon salt
¼ teaspoon pepper
1 tablespoon Worcestershire Sauce
2½ cups water
1 (6 ounce) can of tomato paste
1 tablespoon sugar

Bring to a boil. Lower heat and simmer covered 20 minutes, stirring occasionally.

Hamburger Stroganoff

1½ to 2 pounds ground beef
3 slices bacon, diced
½ to ¾ cup chopped onion
½ cup chopped celery
1½ tablespoons flour
1 teaspoon salt
¼ teaspoon paprika
dash of pepper
1 tablespoon Worcestershire Sauce

2 cans mushroom soup
1 cup sour cream

Cook beef and bacon until browned. Add onion and celery. Cook until tender. Drain the mixture. Add flour, salt, paprika, pepper and Worcestershire to the meat mixture. Stir well. Add mushroom soup and cook on low for 15-20 minutes. Then add sour cream and cook until heated through. Serve over cooked noodles or white rice.

Lasagna Casserole

2 pounds hamburger
1 clove garlic, minced
1½ teaspoons salt
2 cups crushed tomatoes
2 (6 ounce) cans tomato paste
1 tablespoon whole basil
10 ounces lasagna noodles

Brown meat slowly; drain fat; add the rest of the ingredients, except for noodles. Cook the noodles; drain; rinse in cold water.

Cheese filling
3 cups fresh creamy cottage cheese
½ cup grated Parmesan cheese
2 teaspoons parsley flakes
2 beaten eggs
½ teaspoon pepper
1 pound Mozzarella cheese, sliced thinly

Mix all the above except for the Mozzarella. Layer the casserole in a 13x9x2-inch baking dish in this order: noodles, ½ cheese mixture, Mozzarella, ½ meat sauce. Repeat the layers one more time. Bake at 375 degrees for 30 minutes. Let stand 10 minutes to set before cutting and serving.

Mary Berger, aunt

Salisbury Bourguignon

2 cans Beefy Mushroom Soup
1 ½ pounds ground beef
1 egg, slightly beaten
¼ teaspoon salt
½ cup fine dry bread crumbs

3 slices bacon
2 small cloves garlic, minced
¼ teaspoon marjoram leaves, crushed
1/3 cup water
¼ cup Burgundy or other dry red wine

Mix thoroughly 1/3 cup of the soup, beef, egg, salt, and bread crumbs. Shape into 6 patties. In skillet cook bacon until crisp; remove, crumble, and set aside. Pour off all but 2 tablespoons of drippings. Brown patties in drippings. Drain grease. Stir in remaining soup and the rest of the ingredients: garlic, marjoram, water, wine. Cover. Simmer 20 minutes until done. Stir occasionally. Serve over cooked noodles. Garnish with the bacon crumbles.

Ham Loaf

2¾ pounds ham loaf mix
3 eggs
1 ½ cups soft bread crumbs
1 cup milk

Mix the above into a loaf. (If you wish to make your own mix, you will need 1 1/4 pound ground ham, 1 pound fresh ground pork, 1/2 pound ground beef.)

Glaze
¾ cup brown sugar
3 tablespoons pineapple juice
crushed pineapple (opt.)
1½ tablespoons vinegar
3 tablespoons prepared mustard

Heat the above and pour over the meat loaf. Bake at 325 degrees for 1¼ hours.

Florence Lefever, mother-in-law

Company Chicken and Chicken Flavored Rice

6-8 full chicken breast fillets
6 ounces sliced Swiss cheese
1 can cream of chicken soup
1/3 cup white wine

1/3 cup melted butter
1 cup soft bread crumbs

1 cup white rice (not instant)
1 tablespoon chicken bouillon
1 tablespoon parsley flakes
1 teaspoon celery flakes
1 teaspoon dried minced onion
½ teaspoon salt
2 tablespoons butter

Place chicken breasts in a 9x13-inch glass pan. Cover each with a slice of cheese. Mix soup and wine. Spread over chicken and cheese. Mix bread crumbs and butter and sprinkle on top. Bake at 350 degrees for 45 minutes. Combine the rice and the seasonings, adding water and cooking as directed on the package. Add 2 tablespoons butter. Serve chicken over rice.

Linda Berger Kinnee, cousin

Oven Stew

2 pounds lean stew beef
6 medium carrots, cut in 2 inch lengths
2 sticks celery, cut diagonally
1 medium onion, sliced
2-3 potatoes, cut in chunks
1 cup tomato juice
1 teaspoon each, salt and pepper

2 tablespoons Minute Tapioca

Place in large covered casserole in this order: beef, carrots, celery, onion, potatoes, tomato juice, salt, pepper, Minute Tapioca. Cook at least 4 hours at 250 degrees. Can cook up to 6 hours. May also be done in a crock pot.

Lois Weis

Beef Delicious

3 or 4 pounds stew beef
1 (1 ounce) envelope dry onion soup mix
1 can mushroom soup
1 can golden mushroom soup
¾ cup red wine

Mix all ingredients together. Cover and bake at 300 degrees for 4 hours. Serve over white rice. This can also be made in a crock pot.

Fiesta Casserole

1 pound ground beef
¾ cup water
3 tablespoons flour
¼ cup chopped onion
1 (8 ounce) can tomato sauce
1 tablespoon chili powder
3 tablespoons cumin
12 flour tortillas
1 (16 ounce) can refried beans
1 can cream of mushroom soup
1 cup sour cream
2 cups grated Cheddar cheese
1 large tomato, sliced (opt.)

Brown ground beef. Drain. Add water and sprinkle with flour. Stir until thickened. Add onion, tomato sauce, chili powder and cumin. Stir until meat is well coated. Cover and simmer 10 minutes. In a greased 9x13-inch pan, layer 3 tortillas, top with ½ ground meat mixture. Layer 3 more tortillas. Spread the can of beans over them (beans can be warmed in the microwave for easier spreading). Cover with 3 more tortillas and the rest of the ground meat mixture. Mix soup and sour cream. Pour over the top. Top with remaining tortillas and sprinkle with cheese. Bake uncovered at 350 degrees for 40 minutes. Top with tomato slices, if desired.

Texas Chili

2 pounds ground beef
1 large white onion, chopped
½ red pepper, chopped
½ green pepper, chopped
2 cloves garlic, minced
1 large can tomato juice (46 ounce)
1 large can tomato sauce (15 ounce)
2 bay leaves
1 tablespoon cumin
1/2 teaspoon ground coriander
1/2 teaspoon oregano
3 tablespoons chili powder
¼ teaspoon salt
2 cans Bushes red chili beans (mild sauce)
2 rectangular sections Bakers bittersweet
    chocolate

Sauté the ground beef. Drain, if needed. Add the remaining ingredients. Simmer 1-1 ½ hours covered.

Salads

Potato Salad

4 boiled eggs, sliced
5-6 medium potatoes, cooked and diced
1 small onion, chopped
1 cup finely chopped celery
1 tomato, chopped
1 cup salad dressing
1 teaspoon salt
½ teaspoon garlic salt
1 teaspoon sugar (or more, if desired)
1 teaspoon vinegar
1-2 teaspoons prepared mustard
1 teaspoon celery seed

Prepare the first five ingredients. Toss in a bowl. Add the seasonings to the salad dressing. Stir into the potato mixture. Refrigerate for at least 4 hours.

ABC Salad

3 large red apples, unpeeled and cubed
2 cups fresh broccoli, chopped
1 cup dried cranberries
½ chopped walnuts
½ cup canola oil
3 tablespoons lemon juice, divided
1 teaspoon sugar
¼ teaspoon salt

In a bowl, whisk the oil, 2 tablespoons lemon juice, sugar, and salt. Add cranberries; let stand for 10 minutes. In a large bowl, toss apples with remaining lemon juice. Add the broccoli, walnuts, and cranberry mixture; toss to coat. Cover and refrigerate for 2 hours or until chilled.

119

Creamy Coleslaw

2 cups shredded cabbage
3 tablespoons sugar
½ teaspoon salt
3 tablespoons vinegar
2 tablespoons salad oil
3 tablespoons sour cream
celery seed, as desired

Whisk together everything except the cabbage. Pour over the cabbage. Refrigerate for several hours

Kitchen-Klatter Cookbook

Broccoli Cauliflower Salad

1 cup prosciutto, cut into pieces
4 cups broccoli, chopped
4 cups cauliflower, chopped
2 ounces sun-dried tomatoes
¼ pound Provolone cheese, cubed
1 cup mayonnaise
1 teaspoon Grey Poupon, coarse
½ teaspoon sugar
½ teaspoon black pepper
½ teaspoon salt
2-3 cloves garlic, minced
1 cup onion, chopped
basil leaves, dried or fresh, to taste
½ cup olive oil
¼ cup white vinegar

Toss together the first 5 ingredients. Mix the rest of the ingredients together and stir into the vegetable mixture. Refrigerate for before serving.

Brown Rice and Vegetable Salad

2/3 cup brown rice
½ (16 ounce) package frozen loose pack broccoli, corn, red peppers*
2 tablespoons snipped parsley (opt.)
2 tablespoons sliced green onions (if there are no onions in frozen
  veggies)
1 cup leftover roast beef, shredded
2 tablespoons salted sunflower nuts
1/3 cup Italian salad dressing

Cook rice and veggies each according to package directions. Drain both.
Combine all the ingredients; toss to mix in a bowl; cover and chill for several
hours. May be eaten cold or warmed up.

*NOTE: oriental style frozen veggies may also be used.

Vegetable and Other Side Dishes

Party Potato Casserole

8 servings instant potatoes
1 (8 ounce) package cream cheese
½ cup sour cream*
¼ teaspoon garlic powder
butter
paprika

Prepare potatoes as directed. Beat cream cheese and sour cream until smooth. Add potatoes and beat until fluffy. Season to taste with garlic powder. Turn into buttered casserole dish. Dot with butter and sprinkle with paprika. Bake at 350 degrees for 30 minutes.

*NOTE: sour cream with chives may be substituted for plain sour cream.

Green Bean Almondine

3 slices bacon
½ cup sugar
½ cup vinegar
1 medium onion, thinly sliced
2 pounds canned green beans, drained
1/3 cup slivered almonds

Fry the bacon until crisp and set aside. Into the skillet of bacon drippings add the sugar and vinegar. Separate the onion into rings and place in the skillet. Add the drained beans and almonds. Cover and simmer for 25 minutes. Sprinkle the crumbled bacon over the beans when ready to serve.

Marinated Carrots

2 pounds carrots, peeled and sliced
1 onion, sliced
1 green pepper, sliced
½ cup salad oil
¼ cup vinegar
1 cup sugar
1 teaspoon mustard
1 teaspoon Worcestershire Sauce
½ teaspoon salt
½ teaspoon pepper
1 can cream of tomato soup

Cook carrot slices until tender. Cool. Place half of the carrots in a bowl. Separate onion rings and sliced peppers. Place over carrots. Place remaining carrots on top. Mix the remaining ingredients well and pour over carrots. Cover and refrigerate overnight.

Pineapple Baked Beans

1 pound ground beef, cooked and drained
1 (28 ounce) can baked beans
1 (8 ounce) can pineapple tidbits, drained
1 large onion, chopped
1 large green pepper, chopped
½ cup barbecue sauce
2 tablespoons soy sauce
1 garlic clove, minced
½ teaspoon salt
¼ teaspoon black pepper

Mix all ingredients in a 5 quart crock pot. Cook on low 4-8 hours.

Liz Renner

Five Bean Casserole

1 (15 ounce) can yellow beans, drained
1 (15 ounce) can green beans, drained
1 can Van Camp pork and beans
1 (15 ounce) can lima beans
1 (15 ounce) can kidney beans, drained
6 slices bacon
1 medium onion, chopped
½ cup brown sugar
½ cup ketchup
2 teaspoons Worcestershire
1 cup grated Cheddar cheese

Mix all ingredients except cheese together. Sprinkle cheese on top. Bake at 350 degrees for 1 hour or place in a crock pot on low for several hours.

Pat Lefever, aunt

Desserts: cakes, pies, cookies, candy

Chocolate Surprise Cake

2¼ cups flour
1 teaspoon baking soda
1 teaspoon baking powder
1½ cups sugar
2/3 cup shortening
3 eggs
1½ teaspoons vanilla
¼ teaspoon salt
½ cup cocoa
1 cup beer or water
½ to 2/3 cup sauerkraut, chopped, rinsed, drained

Cream sugar and shortening. Add eggs and mix well. Add vanilla, salt, and cocoa. Sift together flour, baking soda, and baking powder. Alternate adding flour mixture and beer or water to the sugar mixture. Fold in sauerkraut by hand. Bake in a greased and floured 9x13-inch pan for 35-45 minutes at 375 degrees. Frost with cream cheese frosting.

Surprise Filled Cupcakes

1 box chocolate cake mix.

Filling
1 (8 ounce) package cream cheese
1/3 cup sugar
1 egg
6 ounces chocolate chips

Follow directions on the cake mix box for cupcakes. Fill the cupcake papers 2/3 full. Beat together the first three filling ingredients; add chocolate chips. Drop a rounded teaspoonful of the filling into each cupcake. Bake according

125

to package directions. Frost as desired.

Waldorf Astoria Red Cake

2 eggs
½ cup shortening
1½ cups white sugar
1 ounce red food coloring
1 ounce water
2 tablespoons cocoa
1 cup buttermilk
2¼ cups cake flour
1 teaspoon salt (omit if using oleo)

1 teaspoon baking soda
1 tablespoon vinegar
1 teaspoon vanilla

Cream eggs, shortening, and sugar. Make a paste of the food coloring, water, and cocoa; add to the sugar mixture. Sift together the flour and salt. Add this mixture alternately with the buttermilk to the sugar mixture. Beat until well mixed.

Dissolve the soda in the vinegar and vanilla; blend into the cake mixture; do not beat. Bake in 2 greased and floured 8-inch layer pans at 350 degrees for 20-25 minutes. Cool the cakes; split into two layers to create a 4 layer cake and frost.

Frosting
Cook the following, stirring constantly, until thick; cool.

3 tablespoons flour
1 cup milk
Cream the following and add to the cooled flour/milk
mixture; beat until creamy.

1 cup sugar
½ cup butter
½ cup oleo

Florence Lefever, mother-in-law

Raw Apple Chip Cake

½ cup oleo
2 cups sugar
2 eggs
2 teaspoons vanilla
2 cups flour
2 teaspoons baking soda
1 teaspoon cinnamon
4 cups raw apples, chopped
1 cup raisins
1 cup chopped walnuts

Cream oleo, sugar, eggs, and vanilla. Sift together the flour, soda, and cinnamon. Add to the sugar mixture and blend well. Add apples and mix slightly before adding raisins and nuts. Bake at 350 degrees for 40 minutes or until a toothpick comes out clean.

Frosting
¼ cup melted butter
¾ cup shredded coconut or nuts
½ cup brown sugar
3 tablespoons cream

Combine all and spread on hot cake. Place under broiler until brown.

Mary Berger, aunt

Never Fail Pie Crust

1 ¼ cup flour
½ cup + 2 tablespoons + 2 teaspoons lard

Cut lard into flour. Make a paste of the following:

3 tablespoons flour
¼ cup water
½ teaspoon salt.

Stir paste into flour mixture. Let dough rest about 5 minutes. Then roll into 2 circles.

Diane Fisher (with modifications)

Bourbon Pumpkin Pie

1 (15 ounce) can pumpkin
2/3 cup brown sugar
1 teaspoon ground cinnamon
½ teaspoon ground ginger
½ teaspoon ground cloves
½ teaspoon salt
¼ teaspoon ground nutmeg
1 (12 ounce) can evaporated milk
2 large eggs
2 tablespoons bourbon

Beat together all the ingredients and place in a pie crust. Cover edge of crust with foil. Bake at 375 degrees for 25 minutes. Remove foil and bake another 25 minutes or until a knife inserted into the center comes out clean.

Lillian Kamler, grandmother

Pecan Chocolate Rum Pie

1½ ounces unsweetened chocolate, melted
3 tablespoons butter
¾ cup dark corn syrup
½ cup brown sugar
3 beaten eggs
¾ teaspoon vanilla extract
1 tablespoon rum
1½ cups chopped pecans

Melt the chocolate and butter together in a heavy saucepan. Set aside to cool. Stir the corn syrup and sugar into the beaten eggs. Add chocolate and butter, vanilla, rum, and pecans. Mix well; pour into pie shell. Cover edge of pie shell with foil. Bake at 350 degrees for 25 minutes. Remove foil and bake 20-25 minutes longer or until a knife inserted in the center comes out clean.

Apple Torte

Bottom
1 cup margarine
2/3 cup sugar
½ teaspoon vanilla
2 cups flour

Filling
2 (8 ounce) packages cream cheese
½ cup sugar
2 eggs
1 teaspoon vanilla

Cream margarine, sugar and vanilla. Blend in flour. Spread into a buttered 9x13-inch pan. Combine cheese and sugar. Blend in eggs and vanilla. Pour into pan and spread evenly.

Topping
5 medium apples, peeled and sliced
1/3 cup sugar
1 teaspoon cinnamon

Combine sugar and cinnamon. Toss apples in the sugar mixture. Spoon into pan. Bake at 450 degrees for 8 minutes, then 400 degrees for 25 minutes. Cool.

Optional Extra Topping
caramel ice cream topping
½ cup sliced almonds

Drizzle ice cream topping over warm torte and sprinkle with almonds.

Dark Chocolate Salted Caramel Oreo Pie

25 whole oreos, crushed
5 tablespoons unsalted butter, melted
8 ounces caramel squares (about 30)
1¼ cups heavy whipping cream, divided
1 (12 ounce) bag dark chocolate chips
¼ to ½ teaspoon sea salt
1 cup chopped, toasted pecans

Spray bottom and sides of 9-inch spring form pan. Finely crush the oreos with a food processor. Stir crumbs together with melted butter until well combined. Press into the bottom and 1 inch up the sides of the pan. Freeze for 10 minutes until set.

Heat caramels and 4 tablespoons cream in microwave 2-3 minutes, stirring every 30 seconds until smooth. Add salt to taste and pecans and spread on the crust.

Heat the chocolate chips and 1 cup heavy whipping cream on high power 1½ minutes in microwave. Whisk until chocolate is melted and smooth. Spread on caramel layer. Sprinkle with sea salt to taste. Chill until set (about 2 hours). Let sit 10 minutes on counter before serving. Remove sides from spring form pan while still cold.

Kevin and Amanda

<u>Cherry Puff Tarts</u>

2 cups flour
1 cup butter
4 tablespoons water

½ cup butter
1 cup water
2 teaspoons almond extract
1 cup flour
3 eggs

1 can cherry pie filling

Heat oven to 400 degrees. Measure 2 cups flour into bowl; cut in 1 cup butter. Sprinkle with 4 tablespoons water and mix with a fork. Divide dough into 12 equal pieces. Pat each piece into a 4½ inch round on an ungreased baking sheet. In pan bring ½ cup butter and 1 cup water to rolling boil. Remove from heat; stir in almond extract and 1 cup flour. When smooth and thick, add one egg at a time, beating well after each addition until smooth. Drop small amounts of batter from a teaspoon to form an edge around each round or use a large star-pointed pastry tube for this edging. Bake 30 minutes; quickly spoon cherry pie filling into each tart. Bake another 10 minutes until puff edge is done. Cool. Top tarts with whipped cream or ice cream, if desired.

Cookie Brittle

1 cup butter
1 teaspoon salt
1 teaspoon vanilla
1 cup sugar
2 cups flour
1 (12 ounce) package mini chocolate chips
1 cup chopped pecans

Preheat oven to 375 degrees. Grease a 12x17x1-inch pan. Cream butter. Add salt and vanilla. Beat in sugar until light and fluffy. Add flour and continue mixing until well blended. Add 3/4 of chips and nuts. Pat into pan. Bake 25 minutes until lightly browned. Drizzle remaining melted chips over the top. Cool. Break into pieces.

Praline Crack

28 whole graham cracker squares
1 cup butter
1 cup light brown sugar
1 teaspoon vanilla
½ teaspoon salt
¾ cup chopped pecans

Preheat oven to 350 degrees. Line a large ungreased jelly roll pan with graham crackers, breaking in half, if needed, to fill the pan. Melt butter and sugar in a saucepan over medium heat until it comes to a boil. Allow it to boil for 2 minutes, stirring constantly. Remove from heat and stir in salt and vanilla. Pour mixture over the top of the graham crackers evenly, spreading to coat. Sprinkle pecans on top and bake in oven for 10-15 minutes until bubbly all over. For a crunchier cookie bake 2 more minutes. Remove from oven to cool. Cut into squares.

Cornflake Coconut Cookies

1 cup brown sugar
1 cup white sugar
1 cup shortening
¼ teaspoon butter flavoring
½ teaspoon coconut flavoring
1 teaspoon vanilla flavoring
2 eggs
2 cups flour
½ teaspoon salt
½ teaspoon baking soda
2 teaspoons baking powder
¾ cup shredded coconut
2 cups cornflakes, crushed

Cream sugars and shortening. Add flavorings and eggs and beat well. Sift together the flour, salt, soda, and baking powder. Add to the sugar mixture and blend well. Stir in coconut and cornflakes. Bake at 350 degrees on a greased cookie sheet for 10-12 minutes.

Kitchen-Klatter Cookbook

Salted Peanut Cookies

½ cup butter
½ cup shortening
1 cup brown sugar
1 egg
½ teaspoon vanilla
1½ cups flour
1/4 teaspoon almond extract
¼ teaspoon baking soda
¼ teaspoon baking powder
1 cup salted peanuts, skins on, coarsely chopped

1½ cups rolled oats
½ cup crushed cornflakes

Cream butter, shortening and sugar. Add egg and flavorings. Sift and add flour, soda, and baking powder. Lastly, add peanuts, oats, and cornflakes. Drop by teaspoons on greased baking sheet and bake for 10-12 minutes at 350 degrees.

Kitchen-Klatter Cookbook

Langues-de-Chats (Cats' Tongues)

This is a typical French cookie, crisp and golden brown around the edges, white in the center, and in the shape of a cat's tongue.

½ cup butter, softened
1/8 teaspoon salt
1 teaspoon vanilla extract
½ cup sugar
2 large unbeaten egg whites
1 cup sifted all-purpose flour

Mix the butter with the salt and the vanilla extract. Gradually blend in the sugar. Add 1 egg white at a time, beating well after each addition. Stir in the flour. Fit a pastry bag or tube with a plain nozzle (# 3). Fill it 2/3 full with the cookie dough. Pipe 2 inch lengths of the dough, 1 inch apart, on buttered and lightly floured cookie sheets. Bake in a preheated 400 degree oven for 6-7 minutes or until the cookies are golden brown around the edges. Cool on wire cooling racks. Store in airtight containers.

Every Day French Cooking

Lemon Gingersnaps

2 cups brown sugar
1 cup shortening
2 teaspoons lemon extract
2 eggs
3 cups flour
2 teaspoons baking soda
1 teaspoon ginger
2 teaspoons cream of tartar
1 teaspoon salt

Cream sugar and shortening. Add flavoring and eggs and beat. Sift dry ingredients together and add to sugar mixture. Blend well. Roll into balls and dip in white sugar. Place on a greased cookie sheet. Bake at 375 degrees for 7-9 minutes.

Kitchen-Klatter Cookbook

Orange Slice Bars

1 pound candy orange slices, cut in 1/8ths
6 tablespoons boiling water
½ cup butter
2 ¼ cups light brown sugar
4 eggs, well beaten
1 teaspoon vanilla
2½ cups sifted flour
2 teaspoons baking powder
½ teaspoon salt
1 cup walnuts, chopped

Pour boiling water over the orange slices and let stand overnight. Cream butter and sugar. Add well-beaten eggs and vanilla. Blend in flour, baking powder, salt, and walnuts. Add orange slice mixture. Bake at 350 degrees for

25-30 minutes in a greased 15x18x1-inch pan. Dust with powdered sugar when removed from oven. Cut into bars.

Chocolate Raspberry Brownies

4 ounces unsweetened chocolate
½ cup butter
2 1/3 cups sugar, divided
1 teaspoon vanilla
5 large eggs
1 cup flour
¼ teaspoon salt
¼ teaspoon baking powder
8 ounces cream cheese, softened
¾ cup raspberry jam

Melt chocolate and butter in a double boiler or microwave. When smooth, add 2 cups sugar and vanilla. Beat in 4 eggs. Add flour, salt, baking powder. Pour one-half of the batter in an ungreased 9x13-inch pan. In a small bowl, combine cream cheese, 1/3 cup sugar, and 1 egg. Mix well and spread over batter in pan. Cover with raspberry jam. Spoon remainder of batter over jam. Bake at 350 degrees for 35-40 minutes. Cool and cut into squares.

Omaha World-Herald, **courtesy of Pearl Schroer**

Chocolate Oatmeal Squares

¾ cup flour
½ teaspoon baking soda
½ teaspoon salt
½ cup margarine
6 tablespoons sugar
6 tablespoons brown sugar
½ teaspoon vanilla

1 egg
1 teaspoon water
1 cup quick oats
½ cup chopped walnuts
1 cup chocolate chips

Sift together the flour, soda, and salt. Cream the margarine, sugars, vanilla, egg, and water. Add to the sugar mixture and blend well. Fold in the oats and walnuts. Spread in a 9x13-inch pan. Sprinkle chocolate chips on top. Bake 375 degrees for 3 minutes. Remove from oven. Using a knife, spread the melted chips into the batter to create a marble pattern. Return to oven and bake 12-14 more minutes. Do not overbake. Cut into squares while warm.

Danish Apple Bar

2½ cups flour
1 teaspoon salt
1 cup shortening
1 beaten egg yolk + enough milk to make 2/3 cup
1 cup crushed cornflakes
4 apples, peeled and sliced
1 cup sugar
1 teaspoon cinnamon

1 beaten egg white

Sift together flour and salt. Cut shortening into flour mixture. Add egg and milk to flour mixture. Don't work it too much. Roll out ½ of dough and put in a jelly roll pan. Press up the sides. Sprinkle the surface with cornflakes. Arrange apples over this. Sprinkle sugar and cinnamon over the apples. Roll out the remaining dough to fit over the apples. Moisten the edges of the bottom and top crusts and press together. Beat egg white and brush on crust. Bake at 375 degrees for 1 hour.

Glaze

1 cup powdered sugar
1 tablespoon water
1 teaspoon vanilla

Mix the above and drizzle on warm pastry.

Simple Sesame Cookies

2 cups softened butter
1½ cups sugar
3 cups all-purpose flour
1 cup sesame seeds
2 cups shredded coconut
½ cup finely chopped almonds

Cream butter in large bowl. Gradually add sugar and continue beating until light and fluffy. Add flour and mix just until combined. Stir in sesame seeds, coconut, and almonds just until well mixed. Divide dough into thirds. Place 1/3 on long sheet of wax paper. Shape into a long roll 2 inches in diameter. Repeat with remaining dough. Wrap and refrigerate until firm. Preheat oven to 300 degrees. Cut rolls into ¼ inch slices. Bake on ungreased cookie sheets 30 minutes. Remove to wire racks to cool.

Omaha World-Herald

Date Pinwheels

1 1/3 cup chopped dates
½ cup sugar
½ cup water
½ cup chopped walnuts
2/3 cup shortening
1 1/3 cups brown sugar

2 eggs
2 2/3 cups sifted flour
½ teaspoon salt
½ teaspoon baking soda

Combine dates, sugar, water, and nuts in saucepan; cook until thick; set aside to cool. Cream shortening; beat in brown sugar. Beat in eggs to mix thoroughly. Sift together dry ingredients; add to creamed mixture and blend well. Chill thoroughly. Divide dough in half; roll each half in a rectangle ¼ inch thick. Spread each with date filling and roll up like a jelly roll. Wrap in waxed paper and chill overnight. Cut dough into 1/8 inch slices and place 1½ inches apart on greased baking sheet. Bake at 350 degrees for 8 minutes. Cool.

Raise-the-Flag Cookies

½ cup butter
½ cup shortening
½ cup sugar
½ cup packed brown sugar
1 egg
2 tablespoons milk
½ teaspoon vanilla
2¼ cups all-purpose flour
½ teaspoon salt
½ teaspoon baking soda
1/8 to ¼ teaspoon red paste food coloring
canned creamy white frosting
blue decorator icing

In a large bowl, beat butter with electric mixer at medium speed about 30 seconds. Add sugars and beat until fluffy. Add egg, milk, and vanilla. Beat well. Stir together flour, salt, and soda; gradually add to butter mixture, beating until well mixed. Divide dough in half. To one half, add food coloring and stir until well mixed. Put waxed paper in bottom and up sides of an 8x4x2-inch loaf pan. Press half of the red dough evenly in pan. Top with half of the plain dough, patting evenly. Repeat red and plain layers. Cover. Freeze at least 4 hours.

Lift dough out of pan by grasping waxed paper. With a sharp knife, slice dough crosswise into three equal parts. Starting at short end, cut each part crosswise into ¼-inch thick slices. Place slices 1 inch apart on ungreased cookie sheets. Bake at 375 degrees 8-10 minutes or until edges are golden. Remove to wire rack to cool.

In upper left hand corner of each cookie, spread a 1 inch square of white frosting. Decorate this square with blue stars, using the blue decorator icing.

Omaha World-Herald, **courtesy of Nancy Byal**

Cranberry Pecan Tassies

Crust
4 ounces cream cheese, softened
½ stick butter
1 cup sifted flour

Combine cream cheese and butter in a medium bowl until well blended. Stir in flour; mix until dough forms. Wrap in plastic; refrigerate 1 hour. Heat oven to 325 degrees. Shape dough into 1 inch balls. Press individual balls into ungreased miniature muffin tins to form tarts.

Filling
1 egg
¾ cup packed brown sugar
1 tablespoon butter, melted
1 teaspoon vanilla
1/8 teaspoon salt
¾ cup chopped raw cranberries
2/3 cup chopped pecans

Beat egg, sugar, butter, vanilla, and salt with a mixer on medium speed until creamy; fill tarts half full. Combine cranberries and nuts in a medium bowl; divide equally among the tarts. Bake until set and lightly brown around the edges, about 35 minutes. Cool in pan.

Omaha World-Herald

Chocolate Covered Cherries

3 (10 ounce) jars maraschino cherries
8-9 cups powdered sugar (about 1 bag)
1 teaspoon vanilla
1 stick margarine
pinch of salt
1 can Eagle Brand condensed milk
2 large bags real chocolate chips
½ stick paraffin wax

Mix and knead (more than bread) the sugar, vanilla, margarine, salt, and milk. Drain cherries on paper towels. Wrap each cherry in the powdered sugar dough. Refrigerate 1 hour. Put paraffin and chips in double boiler. Stir until thoroughly melted. Roll cherries in mixture with forks or toothpicks. Place on wax paper. Marinate in a cool place at a constant temperature for 5 weeks.

"Everything ends this way in France–everything. Weddings, christenings, duels, burials, swindling, diplomatic affairs–everything is a pretext for a good dinner." **Jean Anouilh, French playwright**

ACKNOWLEDGMENTS

It has been my lifelong dream to publish a book. I am very grateful to all who have helped me to accomplish this. First of all, my family contributed in unexpected ways to the success of our new life style. My husband Ken's commitment to the profession of innkeeping was supportive and inspiring. Our three sons prepared me to embrace adventure, sometimes reluctantly, and to adapt to unexpected challenges. Their help with technology in the publishing endeavor was also invaluable. Karen Schotsch, my cover designer, was a professional godsend. Without her expertise I would not have completed this book. I would also like to thank my beta readers: Bill, Jane, Lynda, Teresa, and Cheri. Their helpful suggestions played a huge part in the editing of *Shared Spaces*. Thank you to those whose recipes appear in the book. We have enjoyed eating and serving many of the dishes for years and are pleased to be able to share them in this manner. Indeed, none of this would have been possible without the many guests who slept under our roof and ate at our table. They were the inspiration for the remembering and the recording of our shared time together. Above all I am grateful to God for planting the seed which altered the course of our life journey!

Made in the USA
Coppell, TX
26 November 2020